SAD MAD BAD CHILDREN

By Nicolas Prat. Ph.D.

****

Published by:
Nicolas Prat, Ph.D at Kindle Direct Publishing/Aamazon
Copyright (c) 2014 by Nicolas Prat

****

I0412546

The Demise of Psychoanalytic Theories

In the fifties, psychoanalytic theory had reached a state of quasi-monopoly in psychiatry, a branch of medicine that suffered from a lack of clinical applications. Medications and procedures were rather rudimentary and could not be prescribed for a large number and variety of mild, moderate and neurotic cases that were significant enough to require some form of treatment. Psychoanalysis, created by a physician, filled that need and soon became, as Freud had predicted, the "maid of psychiatry."

With some initial coaxing, psychology eventually shared in the enterprise while developing theories about development, psychotherapy, assessment and diagnosis.

On the whole, psychiatry and psychology shared the treatment and the responsibilities associated with the management of multi-disciplinary teams and policy making. They were working together.

In the sixties, the development of new medications such as tricyclic antidepressant or benzodiazepines, joined with the excess brought about by monopoly began to tear at the status of psychoanalytic theories that had also been widely diversified and expanded by psychological research.

The monolith began to crack and soon to crumble when it became apparent that it could be toppled and the pent up fears and rancor it had accumulated for a variety of reasons flowed freely towards its destruction.

Increasingly, psychiatry had more scientific and medical ways of treating mental illness while psychology also veered towards more scientific metaphors (e.g. data computing) and both began to discard psychoanalytic theories and to replace the foundation and cement they had provided with a so-called "a-theoretical" perspective, meaning the systematic use of statistical theory and its General Linear Model.

The good thing about a model is that, unlike a theory, it cannot be disproved by a single negative result. The trade off, of course, is that it cannot explain anything either. It can only accumulate evidence until, possibly, such a level of accumulation is reached that a statement can be considered as true. From .05 for standard clinical research to five "sigmas" for reaching the status of empirical scientific truth.

A model fosters bottom-up research and discourages top-down approaches, even if all major scientific breakthroughs, including, obviously, the idea rewarded by the 2013 physics Nobel prize, did come from unproven ideas, from top-down theories. It also allows and even funds the moronic studies, regularly encountered in the literature.

As it stands today, psychiatry has fully reverted to its medical, epidemiological roots and psychology has become entirely defined by so-called empirically-validated methods.

The Demise of Psychological Evaluations

The goal of evaluations followed the evolution described above and changed from a conceptualization of each case in psycho-dynamic and historical terms to the formulation of a diagnosis, itself allowing the prescription of a psycho-pharmaceutical treatment. The fourth edition of the Diagnostic Statistical Manual exactly illustrated this aspect by making diagnosis its only goal and the General Linear Model its only tool, as its title clearly indicates.

Following this trend, psychological evaluations shifted their content from conceptualization to fine-grained description of specific sets of signs, symptoms or behaviors with the goal of supporting and fleshing out psychiatric diagnoses.

The enormous amount of experiences and research that had aimed at teasing out of data collected through instruments, particularly projective instruments, clues, patterns and signs of particular dynamics soon lost its use, while diagnostic-oriented instruments became common place.

However, although a solid diagnosis is a good thing for psychiatry as it allows confident prescription of appropriate medication, it is nearly useless for psychology as it does not suggest any particular approach, treatment strategies or tactics for any single case. In addition, diagnostic evaluations have tended to fall victim to a form of trend bias, by which the frequency of a diagnosis increases in function of the availability of a medication or group thereof for that particular diagnosis.

Cases in point are the advent of SSRIs and the corresponding increase in diagnoses of depression, the generalization of psycho-stimulants, and the explosion of the diagnosis of ADHD or, more recently, the availability of anti-psychotics for the treatment of bipolar disorders, the diagnosis of which has increased by a factor of forty (40), in just ten years.

On the whole, such historical development has effectively pushed psychology away from the responsibilities it had once shared with psychiatry and has left it isolated between very territorial physicians and a now rather large number of service providers with lesser, sub-doctoral training and formation. Psychology's attempts at obtaining prescription privileges can only be understood, and questioned, within such context.

The simple truth is that the core of psychology's specific contribution to the clinic is the evaluations it can provide. Its ability to explain and conceptualize a single, particular case, on the basis of data, historical, psychometric or otherwise. This cannot be achieved without resorting to a form of theory and therefore without abandoning at some point or another the quasi-religious fantasy of an objective, pure, empirical stance.

The choice of a theory is basically indifferent, although being conversant with a number of theories, including psycho-dynamic and theories of human development, cognitive, language, biological and otherwise is certainly needed to organize the data in a meaningful way.

If this is done, specific recommendations, both applicable, testable and detailed can be formulated for virtually every single case, thus generating tailored treatment options as well as data that can be used to monitor and further refine treatment. Again, any theory can be used to build such interventions once a hypothesis has been generated in this fashion.

A case conceptualized in psychoanalytic terms can for example inspire a strictly behavioral intervention.

*

Relevance for Children and Adolescents With Severe Behavioral and Emotional Difficulties

One can make a conservative estimate of about 200,000 children or adolescents in residential treatment settings across the United States. Figures are difficult to obtain but many State Medicaid agencies pay about two or three hundred dollars per day for residential placement. Some institutions, for the worst refractory cases, can charge as much as seven or eight hundred dollars per day. As a conservative estimate, these children therefore cost at least about two billion dollars a year.

They also represent a massive business for pharmaceutical companies, particularly since anti-psychotic have been half-approved for the treatment of mood disorders. These atypical anti-psychotic medications do not come cheap and represent a very significant added amount. On the whole, the business of angry children is a multi-billion dollars a year industry.

I used to work in one such residential treatment facility for many years as a staff Psychologist and at some point decided to carry out intake evaluations going somewhat beyond what was required. Instead of a screening for outstanding suicidal, traumatic and substance abuse issues, I decided to attempt to offer a logical explanation for the behaviors, through a narrative merging their life history with data garnered through psychological instruments.

I administered, on average, two instruments, an objective scale of the MMPI or Millon type and a projective instrument, such as the Rorschach. On occasions, when it seemed relevant, I added a cognitive test of the Wechsler family or some other measures.

I was aware that, given the historical context described above, such evaluations were unlikely to result in actual changes to standard treatment routines or in productive discussion with the psychiatrists, but I also felt that it could be beneficial to place in the child's file a document that would at least try to explain the behaviors. I felt, and still feel, that this was indeed my responsibility as a psychologist to provide such a document.

I had set myself the goal of producing an evaluation within the two to three weeks following the child's admission, using the data at hand within this time-frame to put together a best-fit hypothesis about the logic underlying the child's trajectory and clinical presentation.

I also wanted to show examples of how recommendations for treatment could be very specific and derive directly from a psychological hypothesis, rather than general and culminating in a psychiatric diagnosis of little or no use for non-psychiatric clinical practice. In addition. I often made a tactful effort to educate the reader about key concepts or clinical entities so that the conceptualization could be better understood, internalized and the recommendations implemented.

This book is a random collection of a few of these evaluations, thoroughly cleaned of any data that could allow identification of any single individual child and provides the reader with vignettes. There are no research hypotheses, correlative or meta-analytic findings in this purposefully atypical book and I happily let the reader find and build his own version of the big picture of childhood, parenthood, society and the predicament of Psychology, using what these cases communicate as pixels.

I do not pretend, and never have, that the interpretations provided in these evaluations were the absolute truth. I however contended, and still do, that they offer one logical explanation of the child's behaviors, a narrative that attempts to answer the question "Why?" in operational terms. To this day, I still contemplate my dismay when I realized that in over ten years of meetings, staffings and the like, I had never heard anybody asking this question about a child.

As any other, this book is biased by the theories that inspired and structured my understanding and formulation of each case. These theories are psycho-dynamic or psychoanalytical. Freudian, Kleinian, Object-Relations or Attachment-based and are used on the background of an operational knowledge of human development. I chose these theories, in spite of their difficulties, steep and endless learning curve, due to their explanatory power; they are simply the only ones allowing the construction of tailored hypotheses along the entire spectrum of psychopathology. They are the cuisine in a world of fast, processed food.

The excerpts offered are the summary sections. I left out the other sections, particularly the section on psychometric data due to its overly technical and repetitive aspect. I also left out the, often long, section on life history in order to maximize anonymity. An abbreviated version is however given in the introduction to each vignette.

At the end of each vignette, I also wrote a comment that either places the case in a larger perspective, or provides *post-hoc* information. This comment is also often critical, of my own reasoning or of some other aspects suggested by the case.

At the time, it was my hope that some of the individuals involved in the child's treatment, anywhere along the line, would use these evaluations to begin to understand her. It is now my hope that the parent reader will see the way children are always exquisitely attuned to the ones they love, reactive to what happens in their environment and for the most part so surprisingly resilient and responsive.

I also hope that professional readers will agree that although there are biological, genetic predispositions, one can almost always see how what children do and feel makes solid, logical sense in the context of their history. One day, we will probably be able to understand how such context also determines epigenetic changes.

I chose to publish this book through unorthodox channels because it does not fit into standards and also because I do not have the patience or the thirst for external validation required to court publishers who, given the context, are unlikely to see in this work a source of profit or fame.

Finally, if such a view, at least based on children's history and development, was applied across the board, it is likely that there would be much less children in residential treatment and efforts and resources could be focused on those, probably around 10%, who are very severely damaged and actually need it.

I believe that such a qualitative approach would be immensely more efficient than the application of so-called treatment models that essentially aim at maximizing the resources invested through empirical validation of combinations of modalities, leaving the actual content of the therapeutic work for any given individual case to the inspiration, or lack thereof, of under-trained clinicians.

No other discipline than Psychology can meet that objective.

Nobody's Girl

Receiving services since age six or seven, admitted a first time at age nine, this girl was re-admitted for the third time when she was sixteen, which is when this evaluation was carried out.

Placement in a psychiatric hospital was necessary at around age ten, after O engaged in odd, self-destructive behaviors such as climbing on a refrigerator and diving headfirst to the floor.

Placement with mother, grandparents, foster-care all failed and O's level of acting out remained grossly unchanged until her third admission at the same facility.

O is the last child of three. Her father was an abusive, alcoholic hired-hand, occasional rodeo-clown with erratic behaviors and a long legal history starting at a young age. There were reports of this man shooting a rifle from the roof of the house, and of him, while drunk, begging little O to cut-off his penis so he wouldn't have more children.

O's mother eventually divorced when O was about five or six and married another, more stable man, which is when O's behaviors flared up.

O's first placement followed a long series of concerning behaviors of a reckless nature (e.g. climbing on roofs, elopements at night), impulsive (e.g. stealing), relational (e.g. "mean" to siblings, aggressive with peers) and several educational concerns (e.g. hyperactive, under-performing.)

*

Depressive dynamic characterized by a very large guilt component on the background of a pattern of hyper-arousal and anxiety. This background component is thought to have originated in O's early childhood in a very violent and volatile environment where physical, and possibly sexual, abuse was a constant reality.

It is now known that children who have been submitted to or who have witnessed violent situations from an early age tend to develop an hyper-alertness to their environment and a decrease in cerebral opioid activity. As high levels of external stress, including self-harm, have been found to activate the opioids system, a current scientific hypothesis holds that survivors of traumatic situations tend to seek higher external stimulation to counter-act hyper-arousal and achieve a state of relative calm. This result in a quasi-addictive cycle that remains largely unconscious and therefore treatment-resistant as long as its precise causes and mechanisms have not been analyzed and alternative behaviors substituted through repetition.

Reports and observations abound of such behaviors in O since she was brought to the attention of clinicians, at age six or seven.

This psychological substrate has also been, erroneously as far as this psychologist is concerned, diagnosed as an attention-deficit first and then as a manic, so-called "bipolar" component, with which it does however present a number of common signs and symptoms (e.g. apparent mood-swings, occasional restlessness, "hyperness".)

The dominant depressive dynamic appears based on the symbolic loss of her mother who, by all available reports, began to push O away at an early age. This is thought to have originated in O's close and strong bond with a father who was directly, either physically or sexually, abusive to everyone in the family.

Although O certainly experienced her share of abuse, she appears to have represented for her father a sort of *alter ego* and probably witnessed others being abused more and more often than she was herself.

It appears likely that she supplanted her own mother in many aspects of her relationship with her father, which can be easily observed in O's generally poor relationship with women, better relationships with males, whom she regularly claims to have "wrapped around my little finger" (e.g. Residential Supervisor, grandfather, Judge, Guardian *Ad Litem.*)

This state of affairs would have placed O in a position of undue power, particularly for a four- or five-year old caught up in the throngs of the Oedipal conflict, which resulted in the massive sense of entitlement observed today. It would also have dramatically increased the anxiety and the guilt associated with normal aggressive thoughts or fantasies directed against her mother, as her father's abuse of her mother turned them into reality.

Of note is the fact that an actual sexual relationship with her father, which still is a definite possibility, would of course have worsened this situation by further multiplying O's sense of responsibility and her guilt.

Another consequence was to lock O in a double-bind whereby if she is loyal to her beloved father, she betrays her mother and loses her love and if she is loyal to her abused mother, she betrays her father and loses his love.

The clearest manifestation of this conflict can be found in O's documented, systematic difficulties with peer-relations since her earliest socialization and her compulsive insistence at endlessly replicating situations where she will inevitably be blamed for something, while maintaining a way of justifying herself.

It is thought that O expresses in this way a compromise between the two positions described above: by engineering others' hostility (i.e. being mean), she is identifying with her father, the abuser but by getting caught and called on her behaviors she identifies with the victim and has the chance again to protest "I'm being blamed for something I did not do. It's not my fault."

On the whole, she suffers rejection of her same-age peers, makes her life miserable and effectively punishes herself, thereby assuaging her guilt until the next episode.

One can see why O's love for her father has had very limited access, if any, to her consciousness: it amounts to acknowledging her perceived responsibility in the abuse. It also therefore means validating the rejection by a mother she needs and the love of whom she has lost somewhere along the way, during her early childhood as the family dynamics spun out of control or even earlier still, if O was the product of non-consensual intercourse, as it has been suggested.

This is also why O tends to pull away from father authority-figures, which was also observed in her transference to psychologist, as she knows how "dangerous" it can become if she gets too close and uses her "power" on them. Father-figures hit "too close to home". She therefore prefers to associate with younger boys and to look up to unavailable males (e.g. stepfather) or males with a strong motherly, protective component (i.e. grandfather.)

It should be kept in mind that the dynamics described here translated into very concerning self-destructive behaviors in nine-year old O, which provides an order of magnitude to the intensity of her guilt and of the amount of risk she could present in some circumstances and as long as minimal processing will not have taken place.

It is thought that psychotherapy that would not address the issues described above would be inefficient. Disclosure of an unacknowledged sexual relationship between O and her father is still possible.

Diagnostically, the possibility of a Conduct Disorder or, more generally, of an active antisocial component is ruled out although O's manipulativeness and aggressive behaviors certainly could be seen as pointing in that direction. The presence of intense anxiety and of guilt constitutes strong enough evidence to allow this psychologist to feel confident in this contention.

At her age (i.e. nearly seventeen years old) and with her extensive treatment history, it is thought that O would not clinically benefit from a residential placement at this time. It is thought that, in a residential setting and in her context, O's self-destructive behaviors would be likely to flare up and to place her at significant risk of harm with a low probability of clinical gain.

It is thought that a transition placement, such as a Shelter, a Group Home or a foster care family presents a high probability of resulting in elopements, which would therefore expose O to increased risk as well.

The imperfect but optimal option appears to be a probationary placement with her grandparents after a month or two of stabilization, with intensive individual and family psychotherapy targeting the issues described above.

Considering O's pattern of extreme relational difficulties, a placement in the community school system would increase the likelihood of incidents.

Comment

I see in this case as a perfect example of the complexity that often hides behind a series of signs, symptoms and behaviors and of the difficulty of carrying out an accurate assessment. O's presentation contained aspects consistent with ADHD, manic-depression, borderline personality disorder, post traumatic disorder, attachment disorder and she was indeed diagnosed with various combinations of these.

For seven years, she was prescribed various combinations of psycho-active drugs, with no significant effect, aside from the dulling of behaviors obtained through atypical anti-psychotics. So-called treatment-milieu did not impact her either as she seemed to behave like a virus of sorts, adapting to her new environment and replicating the same issues in a slightly different form, but now in a more resistant strain.

I had carried out the psychological evaluation at the time of her first admission and I had then fallen victim to the standard hunt for a diagnosis, giving her a PTSD and a Conduct Disorder. This initial evaluation was perfectly orthodox, and veered away from the obviously inadequate ADHD, but did not provide any indication at all of what were the core, active issues that determined and fueled her ongoing acting out.

Looking back at my second evaluation of O, the one presented here, I still feel a pull towards a manic-depressive dynamic, because her early upbringing with a clearly bipolar and abusive father and a depressed mother would make good sense, even aside from a genetic liability. However, the relational component of her picture was so intense and ubiquitous that such a diagnostic category also feels like an easy way out.

She could also have been put in the broader category of an emerging personality disorder of the hysterical, borderline, antisocial group but she didn't fit snuggly in this category either.

This inability to understand O in the face of unabated behaviors eventually led me to look at her life in a different manner, attempting to extract logic from her relationship and what was available of her family history and dynamic rather than to look for a way to organize her signs, symptoms and behaviors into a diagnostic category.

I knew that, at almost seventeen, she was too old, solidified and eager to be her own self to be amenable to treatment, even if the core issues were finally addressed but I felt the need to at least try to provide a narrative that would be more faithful to her sad story than the labels she had received until then, including that of "criminal" she was now given and started to endorse.

The oscillating, "bipolar", dynamic I constructed in O's evaluation seemed to fit all data in a much more logical and useful way and I have since met several individuals enmeshed in a similar conundrum. I remember in particular a woman in her forties who was close to being admitted to a State Hospital due to what appeared to be manic-like, angry, explosive episodes sprinkled with a multitude of anxious, depressive and psychotic-like symptoms.

Lengthy work in psychotherapy eventually revealed a hysterical dynamic oscillating around a colorful, over-stimulating father and an anxious and controlling mother. Of course this patient had been diagnosed as bipolar. The two poles in question were just her parents. When this dynamic became conscious and minimally worked through, this woman was able to resume a relatively normal life. As hysteria has been thrown away with psychoanalysis, the typical Oedipal triangle has also been discarded but I think that it actually underlies many cases of diagnosed "Bipolar."

At age nine, O could have been freed from her relational prison.

Adrenaline Junkie

Fourteen-year old boy, living alone with his, religious activist, mother. Parents separated when J was very young and he never had much contact, as per mother, with his father, who died accidentally when J was about five. Mother requested help after several months of disobedience and violence in the home and an alcohol overdose. Short, long-hair, muscular Skateboarder initially, J turned to backyard fighting. He reported having been inspired by a tenant of his mother who initiated him to the Martial Arts.

Presence of an emerging counter-phobic personality structure rather than of an isolated clinical syndrome (e.g. "Axis I".)

Counter-phobic adolescents take unusual risks, driving recklessly, taking drugs indiscriminately, engaging in high-risk sexual behaviors and sometimes flirting with potentially suicidal behaviors.

As the name indicates, counter-phobia evolves as a defense against phobia, the obligatory avoidance of specific situations or objects which, although not necessarily dangerous, cause intense anxiety. The counter-phobic individual feels compelled to confront over and over again such objects or situations in the hope, never entirely fulfilled, of obtaining reassurance.

When punctual phobic avoidances become stable, they typically become rationalized as well, thus solidifying into a character structure that becomes increasingly ego-syntonic, further evading awareness and conscious control.

In J's case, the phobic content seems to be related to a pervasive sense of inferiority. J's small size, his lack of a father-figure to oppose, then emulate and grow from, his attachment to his mother, all converged when he reached puberty and probably as early as elementary school, to solidify into an intense fear of humiliation and annihilation and into a phobia of all situations or circumstances, including closeness to mother, that could elicit such dangerous feelings.

Over the years, and particularly as hormonal changes began to take place, J developed his current counter-phobic structure, which directly caused all the behavioral problems of concern.

In particular, it became extremely easy to challenge J to perform any activity that might be painful or contain a significant part of risk (e.g. alcohol, elopement). The mere suggestion will understandably, within the psychological context described here, result in a positive response and a readiness to action. In a way, "the riskier the better."

All other diagnostic categories, such as mood disorder, traumatic etiology, executive problems etc. can be logically and economically subsumed under the emerging character structure described here.

Prognosis is therefore seen as guarded, since characterology is more resistant to treatment, but could improve to fair provided that J's counter-phobic structure reaches a minimal degree of awareness, through verbal articulation, and that sublimation towards productive means begins to be organized. Even if such a result is obtained, however, J is likely to maintain a general counter-phobic character structure but a portion of the energy involved will have been sublimated into socially acceptable and productive means (i.e. dangerous professions.)

Individual psychotherapy should focus on the development of J's awareness of his behaviors and attitudes as defenses against intense anxiety and fear of feeling small, ineffectual, powerless and castrated, rather than as he thinks they are (i.e. proofs of power and strength.) This process should be progressive and tactful as this content is unconscious and as J's sensitivity to slight and perceived put-downs is extremely high.

Family counseling is not indicated at this time, since J perceives his attachment to his mother as a source of the fear of inferiority he tries so hard to ward off. As a result, satisfaction of the first recommendation above is seen as a logical pre-requisite.

On the other hand developing mother's awareness of J's dynamics would probably be helpful, if only because it would provide her with a solid reason for J's hostile behaviors towards her. It would also be important for J's mother to realize that dealing with the psychological structure described in this evaluation, her approach to J's desires, hopes and activities will only be successful if the pressure she applies is not too great. Past a certain point, J will invariably escape control. This type of dynamic is typical of adolescence but in J's case is pushed to a much higher level.

Comment:

My conclusions raised anger in a few people involved in the case, notably a District Attorney of all people, due to the subsumption of the existing psychiatric diagnosis of Major Depressive Disorder to a developing personality dynamic. Interestingly, the psychiatrist was not among these individuals. Following this incident, I decided to completely remove from my evaluations DSM diagnoses and, as much as possible, diagnostic categories as well.

Personality disorders can be defined by the absence of reported symptoms. If symptoms are reported, they typically result from the consequences of the individuals' actions and are therefore not part of the conscious clinical picture. Precisely because of that, they also represent a serious challenge for the psychotherapist, since the participation of the individual in his treatment is never fully enlisted, if at all.

The most accessible of such disorder is the borderline personality, which centers so heavily around relationships that it sometimes allows the psychotherapeutic bond to develop and creates actual symptoms along the way. Treatment is however difficult, stormy and painful, for both the Patient and his therapist and requires thorough knowledge, lots of time and great flexibility to be carried out successfully. Carrying more than one borderline on one's caseload will likely result in increased susceptibility to burn out and Law suits.

Borderline Forever

Seventeen-year old with extensive history of treatment interventions and institutionalizations, starting as early as four or five. Cutting, suicidal statements, occasional outbursts of anger and impulsive behaviors (e.g. shoplifting) during adolescence. Tall, overweight, rejecting of interactions with any males. A's first three years were undocumented but her father reported that she was withdrawn and generally unresponsive when she was returned to him. Sweet food seemed to be her only source or solace. There was also a history of substantiated sexual fondling by the father of A's adoptive mother over a period of a few years during pre-pubertal years.

Data from this evaluation suggested the presence of a borderline personality organization.

Individuals with this type of pathology lead somewhat lonely lives, find difficult to tolerate being alone, are impulsive, non-reflective, and self-preoccupied. They do not clearly distinguish themselves from others and use others to rid themselves of bad feelings or to gratify wishes to feel entirely good. Symmetrically, they also allow themselves to be used by others.

Repetitive frustration, rather than success, is the usual outcome, followed by rage and despair.

Borderline individuals utilize projection and introjection extensively as defenses and demonstrate feelings of hostility and rejection. Psychotic phenomena, often paranoid, are intermittently evident.

This type of pathology is thought to result from a mixture of physiological predisposition, conflict/defense, developmental arrest at the rapprochement phase of the separation individuation (i.e. fifteen to twenty-four months) and/or developmental deviation based on the need to adapt to pathological primary objects.

Such a hypothesis would be consistent with what is known of A's early childhood with an unstable and neglectful mother and would account more thoroughly and economically for her signs, symptoms and behaviors than a manic dynamic.

There also seems to be a strong anal-retentive component which can be observed in a form of stubborn resistance and in a history of retention/explosion cycles which also seems somewhat pleasurable/rewarding to A. Such anal dynamic is also frequent in children who have lived the earliest parts of their life in an unpredictable and erratic environment, as it provides them with a reliable sense of control and with a powerful way of expressing their anger. A's shoplifting impulses can be fruitfully considered within such perspective as well.

It is also likely that A's sexual abuse by the father of her adoptive mother has contributed to her regression to the anal level by blocking a more adaptive resolution to her oedipal phase.

Due to the amount of failure and problems they experience, borderline individuals also typically suffer from depressive symptoms, in particular guilt, low self-regard and an overly pessimistic appraisal of the world and of their future, although these can also be used to manipulate others into accepting their clinginess.

Finally, there were indications that A would be at the upper-end of the borderline range and that she might be closer to a minimal resolution of her problems that her behaviors might suggest. It is even likely that A would regressively but semi-consciously use these behaviors as a way of denying or postponing a rapidly approaching adulthood.

Against all appearances, the above suggests that prognosis could improve to fair, provided that A is not encouraged or validated in her regression.

In psychotherapy, precisely, the best first move appears to question and analyze A's behaviors and general attitude as regression and/or as resistance to maturation. The fact that A's behaviors sharply escalated at around puberty, the first landmark of "growing up" certainly supports this angle.

Such resistance also contains a part of intense and ambivalent attachment to her mother, which her repeated statement of wanting to "find her" expresses on a conscious level. The "object Mother" left abruptly and was erratically present when A was a toddler, which, following the theory, disturbed the development of flexible object-relations.

This aspect will no-doubt be seen in A's transference to her therapist, who will probably experience her as a stubborn, rigid and oppositional toddler. It would be important to keep in mind that such transference really expresses A's fear of and resistance to growing up, which should be systematically interpreted in the early phases of treatment.

A few years earlier, it would have been possible to progressively re-build A's attachment through this transference and the regularity and stability of her therapist but with the few months left before she reaches legal adulthood, it appears realistic to focus on the requirements of reality. In this perspective, it is even thought that focusing on the symptomatic aspects of A's clinical picture, such as her self-harm, could forestall her transition to adulthood.

The above points toward a mixed reality-based, existential and supportive approach for her psychotherapy and to the definition of a set of treatment goals, very concretely organized in a plan with vocational, academic, administrative and life-skills objectives rather than on the behavioral objectives typical of the treatment of children or teenagers.

In the same perspective, A's transition to an open unit should be made as soon as possible, since her staying in the locked unit would contribute to her stagnation by surrounding her with a mother-like holding environment.

Within this context it is also recommended to consider the measures of A's cognitive level with caution. It appears likely that her true IQ is higher than the numbers have indicated so far and that her performance has been significantly impacted by psychological factors. It appears best to consider her highest index score on any given administration as a rough estimate.

Comment

In the absence of tailored interventions, A has continued to follow the same borderline trajectory after she turned eighteen and was discharged back to the community. Stormy relationships with several counselors and brief hospitalizations for suicidal statements. There is always a doubt in the cautious clinician's mind as to the possibility of traumatic etiology in clinical pictures consistent with a Borderline Personality Disorder. However, in A's case the presence of very significant symptoms and behaviors at a very early age and before the molestation had taken place, suggested a personality disorder as dominant psychological complex.

Of course, sexual abuse did nothing to improve her condition but also created an easy explanation for her negative behaviors after she reached puberty.

The presence of sexual abuse issues is likely to have displaced the focus of the clinicians working with her toward traumatic issues, thus leaving untouched the, barely, underlying borderline dynamics, which would in part explain why treatments remained so remarkably ineffective.

After years of treatment, such displacement also left A with the conclusion that what hadn't changed could not be changed and was therefore her identity, thus further validating her personalty disorder.

Incest in the Tomb

Twelve-year old girl admitted following months of open defiance, elopements, cutting, substance use, promiscuity and academic failure. Referral included concerns of psychosis.

Last of three daughters born to a couple who separated when T was just a couple of months old. The children were placed in father's custody. This man was a heavy alcohol and drug user, diabetic as well and could not take proper care of the children so that the older daughter became the caretaker of T. She reported however that T was their father's favorite and spent a "lot of time" with her. T's father's condition deteriorated over the years, including over-doses in front of the children and what seems to have been a semi-psychotic drift away from reality.

Meanwhile, T's mother, who also had serious drug issues managed to pull her life together and eventually regained custody of the children when T was about seven years of age and her sisters teenagers. As T was exhibiting concerning behavior, she was brought to counseling and material began to emerge concerning a likely sexual relationship with her father.

According to O's mother, the case was not brought to trial because O's father died. T's reaction to the death of her father was described as "somber", "tight", with "no emotions" and "no grief". However, she exhibited odd thinking, with thoughts of "unburying her father to look at him".

Over the next few years, T's behaviors steadily deteriorated and included alcohol and drug abuse, promiscuity, elopements, outbursts of violence self-injury and academic under-performance.

Data from this evaluation suggested that T's signs, symptoms and behaviors are psychological sequelae of a sexual relationship with her biological father. The extent and exact nature of this abuse is not known, as it appears that T never articulated her experience but some data, including the early onset of cognitive symptoms (e.g. "learning disability" in Headstart), the apparently intractable acting out behaviors and the presence of primary processes in the clinical picture (i.e. hallucinatory experiences) do suggest a pattern of abuse starting at an early age (i.e. four or five) rather than an acute episode later.

T's "hallucinations", in particular, appear as memories traces of the sexual abuse (e.g. being pressed down in the bed, whispers, hazel eyes) forcing their way out of the unconscious in a symbolized form rather than as *bona fide* psychotic symptoms.

In essence, T's behaviors can be easily seen as enacting a repetition of her abuse and/or of the conditions, including the family dynamics in which it occurred. T's sense of entitlement, repeats her privileged relationship with her father who was "favoring her more". Her anger at being told "No" repeats the sense of all-powerfulness and simultaneous extreme irritation of a five year old whose fantasy of being endowed with the powers of an adult has turned into reality.

T's self-injury also expresses her abuse as the activation of the opioid systems induced by the behaviors counteracts the hyper-arousal and soothes, thus also repeating the body's original response to stress, over-stimulation and ambivalent attachments.

Within this perspective, it also appears understandable that T's behaviors had sharply escalated as she was approaching menarche and as her body began to develop the first signs of sexual maturation; sexuality became impossible to avoid or to ignore and the intense conflicts rooted in T's sexual abuse became very difficult to deny and contain.

Finally, the death of T's father buried the trauma deeper as the internalization of the abuser translated into an increased loyalty to, identification with and possibly idealization of him, thus further defending access to the pathogenic material and creating the conditions for the development of a depressive dynamic.

Prognosis is guarded at this time, for several reasons. First, the likely very early start of the sexual abuse (e.g. first symptoms observed around six) complicates processing. Second, the traumas have remained untouched for a long time and have therefore increased their level of translation into patterns of behaviors and dissociative defenses, making them less ego-alien.

Third, T's father's death has cordoned off access to material related to the abuse, which now requires that he be "un-buried" first, as T powerfully fantasized herself (see dream above, section on Life History.)

It therefore appears that a superficial depressive layer might constitute the best first line of investigation and analysis, which would indeed consist in "un-burying" T's father. As this work proceeds, a genuine depressive reaction is to be expected and it is thought that some time should be spent on processing and grieving without broaching the underlying pathogenic material related to the abuse.

Once the above phase minimally completed, it is thought that access to the pathogenic material related to the abuse will more easily and fluently come forth. At that point, attention should be paid not only to the content but also to subjective manifestations, such as dissociated subjective experiences (e.g. hallucinations), which should be decoded and interpreted. For example, if T relates physical sensations such as sinking in her bed, interpretation of remembering the weight of an adult on her might be attempted. This is deemed important as it contributes to re-establishing logic and reality-testing and therefore to restoring a sense of normalcy.

There is no particular recommendation on a residential or academic level, aside from maintaining identical responses regardless of the phase of T's processing in psychotherapy as she is likely to attempt to use her treatment to indulge her sense of entitlement, which would also represent grist for the psychotherapeutic mill.

Comment

Treatment focused on A's cutting and oppositional-defiance and left other issues untouched. Self-injurious behaviors, such as cutting, seem to absorb many clinician's focus. These behaviors powerfully stimulate the desire or the fantasy to help or rescue while simultaneously providing a clear, measurable objective, a sort of reassuring beacon in a world of unknown and uncertainty.

In truth, although there is no clear correlation between the two types of behaviors, self-injury also frightens institutions as they feel it raises the possibility of suicide. It is also generally "messy" and creates the need of medical monitoring, to prevent infection, transmission and other forms of damage.

As a result, and as in A's case, self-injury often tends to become the problem rather than a mere symptom with little or no consideration given to the psychological cause of the symptom.

In A's case, there were clear indications that self-injury was used as a means to maintain an elevated sensory base-line, itself due to her history of over-stimulation. It was obviously impossible to reach such a deep cause for such an efficient symptom by merely identifying feelings through "chain analysis", remedial actions such as talking to people, breathing and the like.

As usual, treatment limited itself to superficial, reassuring aspects and ignored the larger picture.

Mixed

Tall, friendly and very intelligent sixteen-year old of mixed, Caucasian (Mother) and African-Cari bean descent who was admitted following a year-long severe abuse of cannabis and a recent suicidal episode.

Between seven months and age seven, B was raised by his mother and a step-father who was reported to have been overly "detail-oriented", clean and controlling, traits said to be inherited from a very strict Roman Catholic Eastern European upbringing. These traits sharply escalated after the birth of B's sister, became a form of obsession with "perfection" that was of course never reached and eventually led to a divorce. After the divorce, this man continued his drift towards abnormal, obsessive behaviors (i.e. stalking), which resulted in his US resident status to be revoked. There was no contact between B and his stepfather since.

According to his mother, B developed normally, talked very early and always showed a concern about being "dirty" comparable to his stepfather's.

B remembered that he somehow felt responsible for his parents' divorce, going as far as to think that "if I'm dead, then they'll be able to get back together." This obsession and the irritation caused by the break-up of the family led to a first suicidal gesture (i.e. running towards incoming traffic).

The next years until B's admission followed a pattern of oscillations between relatively normal behaviors and episodes of depression and acting-out, every time resulting in the irruption of suicidal ideation and gestures.

Over these years, B also developed an increasing concern over his identity, starting at around age nine with the question "Was I adopted?" and soon extending to more complex questioning about his bi-racial and multi-cultural history. There seems to have been a general shift from a deep identification with his overly rigorous, white, stepfather and his "rastafari" biological father, whom he never knew but looked like.

Depressive dynamic originating in the loss of B's stepfather, in fact a long time prior to his actual separation from his mother.

B's stepfather appears to have been a major presence in B's very early life but progressively drifted away, with an acceleration at the time of the birth of B's sister, when he was about three or four years of age, also at around the time where object constancy is typically stable.

As this "object" drifted away, B attempted to compensate for the perceived loss by internalizing aspects of his stepfather, including the strong obsessive-compulsive features described by B's mother.

In other words, B's superego structured itself around the template offered by his stepfather's attitudes and behaviors, which included his harsh and exacting requirements for "perfection".

As B's stepfather physically left, the anger at him was naturally turned against the internalized object and therefore against the self as well, resulting in self-punishing, self-destructive acting-out (i.e. first suicidal gesture.)

Such organization makes B especially prone to "situational depression", in which some changes in the environment that have an idiosyncratic symbolic value for the individual develop the impact of an actual loss.

This interpretation would explain why B's conduct markedly deteriorated after he yielded to his friend's pressure to participate in the burglary. B had spoiled the "perfection" demanded by his internalized stepfather and there was therefore nothing left to be saved. A similar all/none, "black and white," thinking is often seen in alcoholics for whom a complete relapse is initiated by a minor violation of their sobriety and in obsessive-compulsive disorders as well, where two opposite wishes endlessly compete for dominance.

B's obsessive-compulsive features are therefore seen as features of his internalized lost object (i.e. stepfather,) rather than constituting a dynamic of its own, and thus as secondary to a depressive complex, which the relative absence of anxiety in the clinical picture does support as well.

It is finally probable that, in a developmental phase where identity formation has become central, B would have then switched his identification to a fantasized biological father, thus initiating an ambivalent vacillation between two opposite poles (e.g. black/white, harsh/loose, emotional/rational.)

Prognosis is guarded at this time but is likely to rapidly improve as/if the depressive complex is processed and with the help of B's excellent verbal abilities.

Comment

In part due to a positive counter-transference and an unconscious attempt at making B's clinical picture more benign than it actually was, I now feel I failed to emphasize the obsessive aspect articulated in a very complex way with the depressive one, in this case and in a couple of rather severe others I came across. In such cases, the obsessive aspect seems to derive from a fixation, a sort of intellectual masturbation that winds up in cyclic behavioral discharge.

Transference and counter-transference are very active for psychological evaluations as well, including cognitive evaluations and are often underestimated, assuming that such notion is even recognized by the evaluator.

Retrospectively as well, I think that B's symptoms flared up when he reached a developmental phase where the definition of an identity was central and therefore brought up and exacerbated all the tensions and conflicts between racial identity, gender identity, moral identity that had been mostly latent up until then. B's extensive cannabis abuse at adolescence and up to his admission was also probably an attempt at identification with his biological father and to escape and negate his stepfather's rigid control as well as a way of alleviating the constant pressure of a harsh super-ego.

The presence of an obsessive aspect to some depressions, as in B's case, remains unclear to me, in part because I have seen only two or three of such cases. These cases were always very severe, with phases of obsessive thinking or brooding followed by what seemed like impulsive acting-out with partial loss of reality-testing abilities.

I still don't think that a manic reaction is the correct interpretation, mostly due to the nature of the obsessive brooding, which is not accelerated or flighty but circular, as it were, reminding of a software stuck in a loop, to the presence of guilt and magical thinking and to the undoing that acting-out typically represents for the individual.

I think that these brooding/acting-out cycles can be best conceptualize as a symbolic repetition of an anal cycle of retention/explosion or possibly even refer to an earlier oral dynamic.

Burnt Out Mom

Ten year old boy admitted from a psychiatric hospital from a foster-placement where he had displayed severe enuretic and encopretic behaviors and made suicidal statements. K had been removed from his home along with four younger siblings following mother's neglect and allegations of abuse.

K is the oldest of five boys born to a married couple, the youngest was about a year old when the mother began to drift away, "hanging out with teenagers" and becoming generally neglectful. Mother's became increasingly neglectful, leaving the children unattended for extended periods of time and there were substantiated allegations of fondling of the boys, which resulted in her being incarcerated. The children were placed in foster care and K's behavior that had already flared up when his mother had begun to drift away, sharply escalated and included severe enuresis and encopresis.

Data from this evaluation converged in suggesting the presence of a simple depressive dynamic rooted in the symbolic loss of the mother, who apparently became overwhelmed and decompensated as her five children, all boys, became more autonomous and less dependent on her.

Secondary data suggested that K's mother might have unconsciously fantasized her children as living dolls surrounding her with warmth and a sense of purpose as her husband was typically absent.

It appears that she would have turned away from her children, possibly blaming them for "leaving" her and punishing them accordingly, including by leaving them in return.

From K's perspective, this shift was equivalent to a serious loss since his mother had been caring, mostly stable and present prior to such shift. The fact that K's father was absent, working nights, year after year, left him without a reliable male figure and with an increased sense of his responsibility.

When K's mother drifted away, her introject kept on punishing K from the inside following the classic schema of depression, while the good part of the introject (i.e. the ancient benevolent mother) made, and makes, extremely painful for K to grieve her loss.

The resulting conflict was dampened by K through regression to the anal stage, the latest successful developmental stage, expressing simultaneously the unconscious wish of being taken care of (i.e. cleaned, changed,) of evading the overwhelming Oedipal fantasy of taking care of the mother like the father does and the wish of retaliating against his mother for her "leaving".

On the whole, K's symptoms, signs and behaviors appear to be the direct product of his despair at having lost his "good enough" mother, devastating thoughts and feelings that are therefore powerfully repressed and dissimulated being a wall of anger. It is thought that such loss is so wide and deep that it supersedes the abuse and the neglect endured by K, the shame associated with his situation and the sadness at being separated from his family.

Although tests data did not provide clear support for it, the presence of anxiety, most probably of an Oedipal origin but also secondary to the depressive dynamic, is suspected in K's clinical picture and expressed through restlessness and hyperactive-like signs, symptoms and behaviors.

Prognosis is however deemed fair, due to K's relatively mild level of behaviors, to his good intellectual ability and to the relative resilience evolved from an acceptably stable early childhood.

It is thought that abreaction of K's pain at having lost his mother will be enough to alter the course of his depressive dynamic. Verbal processing and working through should then solidify insights into stable behaviors in a relatively short period of time.

However, patience and tact will be needed before reaching the point where K will be able to let go of his anger as a defense and to experience and acknowledge his pain. Focusing on the resistance (i.e. anger,) including in his anal forms, therefore appears as a logical priority.

Family counseling is not recommended until the above goals have been minimally met, which should be left entirely to K's counselor's judgment. If administrative or insurance requirements impose a form of "family therapy", it is recommended to keep the exchanges at a minimum of intensity and to avoid focusing in family sessions on the above issues before they are reasonably processed individually.

Doing otherwise is likely to be detrimental to the course of the treatment, for example by running the risk of encapsulating the problem.

No particular recommendations is made as far as the residential aspect of K's treatment, but staff might be alert to the fact that mixed male/female consistent and simultaneous presence and interventions are likely to be very reassuring to K, particularly if/when he is upset.

This evaluation indicated a central depressive dynamic and thus supported the current prescription of an anti-depressant.

Comment

This case illustrates a category I see in many young mothers, who emotionally and sometimes physically disappear when their children show the first signs of becoming autonomous. The fantasy of "having babies" and the fact that infants are easier to live with than toddlers hold these mothers in place for about eighteen months but quickly dissolves after that. Another pregnancy sometimes resets the counter but reality eventually catches up. K's mother did not have any choice aside from decompensating, "cutting loose" as it were, all the more since she was reported to fall within the Borderline Range of intelligence.

There is also a real underestimation of what mothers of two or more children, close in age, and of low income have to go through when the husband is out earning the household's income. Some husbands even stay longer than they have to out of the home as it allows them to preserve their freedom, a sort of ownership of their wife and family, while maintaining a sense of righteousness. Women do not have this luxury. Most weather the storm but some, the more unstable or fragile, do decompensate, sometimes severely.

This case also illustrates the use children make of feces as a weapon, as an expression of anger and as a way of controlling or manipulating their environment. I have seen foster-adoptive parents "returning" their child soon after the cute little thing they thought she was had begun to express her ambivalence in this way. Instead of being neutralized, the power of feces is regularly confirmed and validated by the reaction of the environment, including in treatment facilities or specialized foster-care settings. Which is why children use it so much.

The Caretaker

Fourteen-year old girl who managed to maintain an acceptable level of performance in the school, aside from an increasing number of tardies or absences. Generalized disobedience in the home and physical altercations with family members, including father. Was admitted to a psychiatric hospital at the end of the school year, after having made suicidal statements, which she reiterated during her intake session with the admitting physician. Discharged a couple of weeks later, G returned to her home and received counseling but attempts at providing her with more structure through outpatient services failed.

Data from this evaluation suggested the presence of a dysthymic disorder originating in the symbolic losses incurred by G about four to five years ago, as her father drifted off toward extra-marital relationships and her mother into a depressive and hypomanic state which included a suicide gesture and required a brief psychiatric hospitalization.

At that point in time, G also symbolically lost her childhood and gained the responsibilities of an older member of the household as she had to increase her participation in the care of her older developmentally disabled brother and of her younger brother as well.

Since then, G's family situation has remained in a state of relative stalemate, with her parents recurrently fighting and attempting to reconcile, occasionally seeking support outside of the home, or in alcohol, in G's father's case.

Data suggested that G's dominant loss in this context has been that of her father, which she attempted to compensate by becoming "boy crazy" early on. Regression to the mother was made impossible by mother's unavailability, thus leaving G feeling betrayed, angry at her parents and at her responsibilities (e.g. her dream.)

As G's ambivalence about being the family's care-taker increased, so did the amount of guilt and of anxiety she experienced which she attempted to resolve by ambivalently leaving the home, as nicely illustrated by her elopement with her mother's car (i.e. running out of fuel.)

However, G's guilt proportionally increased with such attempts, suggesting that the dysthymic dynamic would run deeper than a chronic adjustment disorder. The amount of G's guilt was evidently expressed in her suicidal ideation, which along with other data pointed toward the possibility that G would have been unconsciously invested with the responsibilities of a mother-figure, at first on a symbolic level, since a very early age or even since birth (i.e. the only daughter), due her parents' erratic dependency needs which were likely present before they started to drift apart.

Children invested with such "responsibilities," unconsciously projected into them by dependent parents become excessively guilty as the implicit requirements always fall a long way beyond what they can realistically provide, which leaves them in a permanent state of "failure" very conducive to developing stable depressive dynamics.

Prognosis is deemed fair at this time and with this very verbal young lady with a mild level of acting out.

It therefore appears that psychotherapy has several potential targets and it is recommended to organize them by level of depth, starting with G's sense of abandonment by her father, when she was seven or eight, which seems to be closer to the surface.

The second goal of acknowledging and of verbalizing her anger at being burdened with the responsibilities of a caretaker could become rapidly available, following which her fantasies of being the "Mother" could become accessible. Guilt and anxiety are likely to appear at this stage.

This would lead the way to a last, deeper, level which would reach G's dysthymic core, inherited from her mother's dependency issues and which would consist in examining the mother-daughter dyad.

Of course, family psychotherapy should follow the unfolding of these objectives and begin only when minimal insight has been acquired in individual sessions (…)

Comment

The dream mentioned above was a nightmare she brought up at intake, during which her parents and younger brother were being killed. As I observed that her older brother was not in the dream, G explained that "he is developmentally disabled, he is innocent. He doesn't deserve to die." Immediately realizing the meaning of what she had implied (i.e. that the others did deserve to die), G spent the next several minutes explaining that she didn't it mean this way but that way and so forth.

Dreams brought by adolescents are often very superficially encoded, which is probably also why they seldom remember them or care to elaborate when they do remember them.

This other fourteen-year old girl with significant traumatic issues, anxiety and high levels of unconscious anger at her mother had dreamed that her mother had been in a car wreck and was stuck upside down in her car that had flipped over. During previous sessions with psychologist, she had insisted on listening to a rap song she loved and whose motive was "I'm gonna pick up the World and drop it on your fucking head". Psychologist interpreted to her that in her dream, she had effectively done just that (i.e. inverted position in the car). In this case as well, the content was readily available to low-level interpretations.

Contemporary Hysteria

Sixteen-year old referred by her school district who was concerned by increasing levels of anger, defiance and what appeared to be depression. H was also at extreme odds with her mother and her mother's family. She had been adopted as an infant and grown extremely close to her father who had died when she was about thirteen years of age. Since that time, she had become increasingly aggressive and defiant and had also engaged in a suicidal gesture, which did motivate her family to build a case for long-term admission, with the help of the , terrified, local school district.

Data from this evaluation converged in suggesting a primary anxiety disorder with marked phobic features and a secondary, reactive, depressive disorder.

The core of H's clinical picture is therefore thought to be relatively resilient with a central neurotic conflict revolving around Oedipal issues amplified by H's privileged relationship with her father since a very early age.

Since a very early age as well, there seems to have been strong counter-phobic defenses, which consist in seeking the feared situation, usually a symbolic substitute thereof, in order to assuage and/or control the anxiety (e.g. mountain climbing/fear of height.)

Within this perspective, H's hyper-sexuality can be understood as a expressing a conflictual and anxiety-ridden fear of sexuality, and possibly of a loss of control, rather than what it appears to be.

The same logic would also apply to H's need to show her body, as exemplified by her semi-obsessive and very early fantasy of becoming a model, which would express her exhibitionistic attempts at warding off the anxiety of being "ugly" or "incomplete."

Similarly, H's suicidal gestures by drowning evidently appear as counter-phobic to her phobia of large bodies of water, which is often expressing a fear of merging with/in the mother and therefore refers to an aggressive or ambivalent relationship to her.

The exact dynamics and meaning of H's phobias belong to her psychotherapy but her counter-phobic defense appears as central to the behaviors that led her to residential level of care.

The second element of H's clinical picture, as supported by the data garnered through this evaluation, is a depressive component, based on several losses starting in 2001 with the death of her paternal grandmother and culminating about three years ago with the diagnosis of her father with an aggressive form of cancer from which he died less than a year later, when H was about thirteen years of age

The onset of the depressive component suggested that the death of the grandmother represented the fulfillment of an Oedipal unconscious aggressive wish against the mother, thus initiating, through guilt, a depressive pathology rather than a normal grieving.

The death of her father a few years later solidified H's depressive dynamic, with the secondary gain of offering an easy and convenient explanation to H's every sign, symptom or behavior, while intensifying an unresolved Oedipal conflict.

H's suicidal gestures can be seen as nicely summarizing the above complex dynamics; thinking about her dead father stimulated the aggressive unconscious wish against the mother (i.e. "You, should have died not him"), while guilt demanded proportional punishment (i.e. death) and retaliatory atonement, realized through the choice of means (i.e. drowning = symbolically merging with mother.)

The fact that death by drowning is and was very unlikely, particularly in a tub, also suggested the presence of a depressive fantasy, a make-believe of sorts, rather than that of a bona fide self-destructive acting out.

H's ambivalent relationship to her mother also seems to tie in a form of eating disorder of the anorexic spectrum, itself tying in the "model" complex and its counter-phobic aspect. Sometimes, for example, girls become obsessed about not gaining weight, and therefore will starve, as a symbolic way of denying/countering the development of their body's secondary sexual characteristics.

In addition to expressing such phobia of womanhood, girls' anorexia also often represents a symbolic form of aggression/rejection of the mother (i.e. food).

On the whole, prognosis is considered fair at this time, due to the neurotic level of H's pathology and to her above average intelligence level and verbal abilities, but is of course dependent upon the extent to which the unconscious conflicts underlying her current clinical picture will have been processed, verbalized and worked-through.

H's phobic formations present themselves as the best point of entry in her dynamics and should be focused on initially. The mechanism of phobia/counter-phobic behaviors should be discussed and elaborated upon, with the goal of making H's negative behaviors more alien to her but also more comprehensible, therefore initiating deeper processing and change.

It is recommended to postpone work on the depressive aspect until insight has been acquired on the above, in large part because it would probably be used as a resistance and a universal explanation for everything without necessity to develop insight into more pervasive dynamics. In addition, as described above, this aspect would tie in H's guilt and her relationship with her mother, which connects too directly to deeper issues.

For similar reasons, it is recommended that mother/daughter psychotherapy be postponed as well, until minimal insight has been acquired by H and failing which, sessions are likely to harden the resistance. Casual, superficial contacts are not a problem, with the goal of having mother and daughter have a non-confrontational, courteous, "minimal" conversation.

H is highly likely to trigger powerful negative counter-transference reactions in female staff, including her therapist, and work should focus on her own, mostly unconscious, negative transference onto female authority figures. This aspect should be broached slowly and with tact, or it would be used as a confirmation of the therapist's hostile intentions. Rather, H's psychotherapist should reassure her by demonstrating that she can tolerate her aggression. Material derived from this aspect would of course be extremely useful later on, when Oedipal aggression towards the mother would be processed.

No particular recommendation is made as far as residential interventions and the standard model should work fine with H, although interactions with female staff could become tense and conflictual at times for the reasons exposed above.

Comment

It appeared quickly to me that H had more or less consciously engineered her admission away from her family, precisely as a way of forcing her will upon her mother. This does not mean that she did not have psychological problems but that such problems were relatively mild and could have been addressed on an outpatient basis. However, given the lack of psychologically savvy and/or trained counselors in the area, a small town in a rural, under-served, State, an inpatient admission became an easy manipulation for this intelligent hysterical girl.

On a larger scale, it has been my observation that a very large number of teenagers I met since around 2000 in this rural State and in different clinical settings ranging from clinics to State Hospital, at least in part resorted to such planning to escape, if provisionally, their environment. They quickly learned the key-words, suicidal in nature, that were likely to have the desired effect.

In fact, I would go as far as suggesting that this was the case in about 99% of all the adolescents I met. The remaining 1 percent were actually in real danger of killing themselves and about all of them, that I know of, eventually did.

Taking threats seriously is good but the flaw resides in the evaluation process. Few clinicians, including psychiatrists, will privilege a false positive over a false negative and those who do generally have a theory to ground their judgment. In those days where theory, aside from statistical theory, is considered as "noise" spoiling the data and where resources are scarce, the evaluation process suffers and so does the selection ratio. The very same process takes place with homicidal presentations.

Forty years ago, a social-worker in psychoanalytic practice would have treated this case in a few months and in the community. Today, it took a team of at least twenty people and a residential stay of several months to interrupt H's acting-out without reaching any kind of resolution.

Oedipus in Exile

This fourteen-year old boy was admitted following over a year of opposition and defiance of all the rules in the home and in the school as well. There was also a history of suicidal statements and two brief stays in residential settings, one in a psychiatric hospital for "stabilization" and one in a local structured Group Home, which resulted in further escalation of negative behaviors and led to his admission for long-term treatment.

Data from this evaluation suggested the presence of a psychological problem best described as a chronic adjustment disorder. The initial stressor is thought to have been Z's symbolic loss of the exclusive relationship he had with his mother for about three years after his parents' separation when he was about four.

Although adjustment disorders are typically short-lived (i.e. a few months), while the individual learns to adapt to the new situation, it can become chronic in some cases where the individual cannot, for a variety of reasons, process the stressor or when the stressor itself is chronic.

In Z's case, the chronic factor is thought to have been the very intense anger at having been deprived of his "Oedipal triumph", the sense of omnipotence that develops when the child wins over the parent of the opposite sex, due to death or other forms of disappearance or collapse of the same sex parent.

As Z was about seven and within a couple of years, his mother met and married her current husband and gave birth to their first daughter, while Z's father remarried as well, leaving Z a mere subject in a larger family.

The narcissistic injury sustained in such circumstances and the large amount of resentment and anger that results take different forms depending on each child's particular circumstances but typically amounts to a retaliation on the parents, particularly on the opposite-sex parent.

The means used by the child to that end unconsciously express both the child's love and hate for the parent(s), the hate through spoiling what is the most valued by the parent, for example school performance, the love through emulation of the parent(s) mode of reacting to stress, for example by mimicking the parent(s) depressive tendencies.

As clearly suggested by the data, Z began by spoiling his school work, probably an attack on his father who reportedly values Z's school performance, and increasingly endorsed a depressive *persona*, probably an attack on his mother by threatening to hurt himself as a sure way of hurting her, and possibly as an imitation of her own depressive tendencies. Also, as Z learned very early on, his hurt tends to bring his mother physically back to him (e.g. migraines.)

Z's most recent escalation, the "horrible" eight grade, was in part boosted by the onset of puberty and the influx of testosterone, the hormone of aggression, multiplied by the normal adolescent re-hashing of past developmental crises.

Z's angry and hurtful statement to his girlfriend that he was going to kill himself because of her cheating on him constitutes a clear and simple summary of such dynamics.

Prognosis is deemed fair at this time, since Z's depressive mood appears to be more reactive and circumstantial than essential and since data also suggested a relatively well-structured Ego. However, this will of course depend on Z's ability to come to terms with the neurotic conflict described here rather than to regressively acting it out.

Psychotherapy could focus on the hypothesized origin of Z's current symptoms, the time where his life as an only child, alone with his mother ended. Z is likely to claim difficulty remembering but such attempts should however be made, possibly through sessions with his mother where this important phase of their life would be reminisced.

The sense of power and of control that Z derived from his migraines since an early age could be discussed, analyzed and compared to Z's current regressive strategies, which are very similar in many respects. Essentially, Z's depressive *persona* ala Kurt Cobain could be interpreted as a regressive attempt at forcing his mother back to rescue him.

Z's willful academic failure should be explored, possibly with his father, as a means of hurting him and therefore as a means of expressing anger at him while generating comparable anger in him.

Family psychotherapy, equally important with mother and father, is therefore seen as a productive component of Z' treatment.

The existential crisis of adolescence as the loss of childhood could be explored as well with some benefit and Z's behaviors could also be interpreted within this perspective as attempts at denying such loss masked by "grown up" content and fantasies (i.e. going to Los Angeles.)

The hypothesis offered here does support the use of substances as an anti-depressant but also, and mostly, as a way of making fantasies, and identity, more convincing; as an accessory of sorts.

Data from this evaluation and the above hypothesis could inform a different, possibly lighter, approach to Z's pharmaceutical regimen.

Comment

This case always seemed to me to provide a good illustration of the often terrible fourteenth year boys go through. Even in the absence of significant psychological problems this fourteenth year sits exactly at the border of childhood and adulthood territory and the increase in aggression and libido due to the hormonal rush will turn any boy, at least once in a while, into a disturbed individual. When there are significant underlying problems, including severe ones, they are multiplied. For girls the same seems to take place a year earlier. For both, unsurprisingly, these are the years where substance abuse often begins.

This case also brings to mind another way in which children express anger towards their parents, by failing academically. Until around age sixteen, children do well in school not for themselves but simply to please others. Although there are variations following the importance educational success has in the family, a sudden drop in the child's academic performance, in my experience always signals a problem and the child's anger at one or both of his parents.

The older the child, the more serous the problem and the deeper the anger, because it shows a wider discrepancy between the child's normal developmental level, his growing autonomy and the regressed nature of the behavior.

I had a sixteen-year old boy, probably above average, excellent in math and who was admitted by his school district due to academic failure. The boy was not only under-performing, he was squarely refusing to go to school and was about to repeat his grade or even to jeopardize his course towards graduation. His mother, with whom he was leaving alone, was a Kindergarten teacher, working in a town about one hour away from their home.

Everybody's Barbie

D was born from a temporary relationship and very little is known about pregnancy and infancy. D's mother was a troubled young woman who has mothered another girl in similar circumstances about a year earlier.

D's history comes into focus when she was about three years of age, as a report for neglect was filed to the local Human Services. At that time, D was living in a sort of "commune" with numerous adults and very young children, including her one-year older sister. The conditions in the house were extremely concerning (e.g. extreme disorder, promiscuity, large amount of cat and dog feces, lack of supervision) and D and her sister were taken into State's custody, where they remained for the next two or three years, after numerous attempts at bringing her mother and stepfather to a minimal level of consistent compliance and responsibility.

D's stepfather was also suspected, as per D's sister's report, of repeated sexual abuse, all circumstances that eventually resulted in D's parents' rights to be relinquished/terminated and in the children being adopted.

D was adopted, individually, by her current family and appeared to bloom in her new environment. However, starting about seven to twelve months ago, or around her eight's birthday, D began to display odd behaviors, such as urinating on clothes in her room, urinating on rolls of toilet-paper, defecating in a container and hiding feces under her bed.

Soon, D began to elope from her home, sometimes at night, on occasion preparing a backpack and planning her elopements. On a few occasions, she succeeded and, once, was found hours later in the company of strangers, older men with whom she behaved in an overly friendly manner.

Behaviors were also observed to degrade in the school setting, thus describing a general deteriorating trend that soon was deemed unmanageable by her adoptive parents. A placement at a local psychiatric hospital was decided and long-term placement recommended.

D's adoptive mother reported that she could not identify any meaningful change in D's life at around the time of her behavioral escalation. She however remembered that a year prior to that, at around D's seventh birthday, contact with her sister, who had been adopted separately, were in effect severed. D's sister had been invited to D's birthday party but did not come.

D's adoptive mother also mentioned that D's biological mother had begun delivering newspaper to their home but that neither mother nor daughter seemed to have even recognized each other.

Data garnered through this evaluation suggested a clinical picture superficially dominated by features consistent with an attachment disorder. It is important to note that attachment disorders vary along a very wide continuum ranging from psychiatric conditions of "failure to thrive", anaclitic depression, or "hospitalism," sometimes leading to attrition and death, to adjustment disorders belonging to the neurotic range, as happens for example when divorced parents maintain a conflict around their children.

In the view of her relatively pathogenic early upbringing and of her symptomatic expression, D appears to be located somewhere in the middle, at a point where pathogenic circumstances began to affect cognitive and sensory development. Exposed to chaos in terms of noises, smells, emotional modulation and stability of care, while possibly equipped with good innate sensory responsiveness, D has developed a high baseline, below which sensory stimuli do not fully register.

Even if D's has since lived in much more stable environment (e.g. foster care, adoptive home) and has markedly improved, she is still too young to have developed and consolidated all the neural structures involved in this process.

In fact, it is thought that the behaviors observed in D over the past year are a regressive reaction to the deep changes that consistent care has begun to make and at a time where, approaching the end of childhood and the beginning of pre-adolescence, children also tend to regress towards their mother.

The physical re-appearance of her biological mother (i.e. delivering paper at her home) and the disappearance of her sister (i.e. adopted separately) is thought to have multiplied D's difficulties as it triggered unresolved attachment issues.

It is very common, if not systematic, to see in foster or adopted children occasional rises in ambivalent attachments as the discrepancy between their caring homes and parents and the historical bond with their biological parents increases through crises or accidental circumstances. Contrary to the intuitive belief, the bond between a child and abusive and/or neglectful parent (s) is much stronger than it would be in the absence or adverse circumstances and these children tend to be subject to very intense conflicts revolving around loyalty and identity.

Within such hypothesis, D's behaviors would be meaningful in the following way: running away symbolically expresses an unconscious wish to run to her mother "somewhere in town", and to run away from the good life she has in her adoptive home. Urinating and defecating in her room expresses an unconscious wish to regress to a period where her room was indeed covered in urine and feces.

The bodily products also symbolically represent D's childhood and she expresses the unconscious wish to keep it by storing them (i.e. urine in paper-roll, feces in bowl).

As exposure to sexual activity, at least as a witness, is highly likely in D's early, pre-adoption, history, a sexual component in her acting out is thought to have a similar regressive meaning more so than the repetition of an actual abuse on herself.

More generally, all such behaviors also "spoil" D's good life, in this way making it less desirable and correspondingly reducing its discrepancy with her past life.

Unconsciously again, and as neglected children are typically very protective, D might also feel anxious about her mother's current state and health.

However, it is also thought that D's current signs, symptoms and behaviors, in particular their diversity and occasional odd aspect, manifest a deeper depressive dynamic with manic defense, by which the loss is denied and a state of "re-fusion" with the lost object takes place. This deeper dynamic, also consistent with D's unstable infancy and early upbringing appears to be mild in intensity, cyclothymic rather than bipolar.

It is recommended that psychotherapeutic treatment focus on the outermost layer of her dynamics, the disorder of attachment. A primary target therefore appears to be D's fantasies about her biological mother, which will probably be only possible to reach through play and/or projective activities, as such fantasies are in large part unconscious.

It will be more productive to go to a calm and empty space with a few chosen toys rather than in the play-therapy room, where the number of available objects is likely to rapidly over-stimulate D and to fuel her hypomanic restlessness.

Painting, finger painting or sculpting with putty (i.e. substitute for feces) could provide a measure of productive regression and facilitate symbolization and verbalization.

Interpretation to D of her behaviors along the lines suggested above might also be helpful in establishing a productive communication with her and bring to her conscious attention the intense conflicts she is experiencing.

Family therapy with D's adoptive mother is not recommended until minimal processing of D's ambivalence between her mothers has been achieved. In the mean time and if contacts are imposed by insurances' administrative requirements, it is recommended that sessions consist of light, friendly chat and avoid deep conflictual issues.

It is likely that D's placement constitutes a reprieve for her, as she is in a "third", neutral, home environment probably reminiscent of her earlier years in the local foster-care system. This regressive aspect facilitates her treatment at this time but an increase in behaviors might paradoxically be observed as the conflict described above wanes.

A positive indicator of D's therapeutic gain would be the emergence of a depressive reaction. This would signal that the grieving of her losses has begun and that her hypomanic denial has lost its grip. This phase is not seen as a *sine qua non* condition of her discharge. It will remain an important dynamic to analyze and is likely to extend well into adolescence, as issues of identity will take center-stage.

Comment

A few weeks after her admission and this evaluation, it appeared that D's adoptive family had in fact been on the path of disintegration for a few months before she started to act out. Her mother, in particular seemed to develop an alcohol abuse problem and engaged in on-line relationships, essentially abandoning D emotionally as her biological mother had done in the past.

I had erroneously explained the onset of her behaviors and signs as an attempt at spoiling a good relationship, when, in reality, this relationship had already been spoiled, by merely repeating a pattern very familiar to D, abandonment. This became also quickly apparent as her adoptive mother missed nearly all of her phone sessions with D, which left her with no family, no one to talk to aside from her social-worker and residential personnel.

Nearly a year after her admission, D, whose behaviors certainly did not justify a placement at the highest level of care, assuming they ever had, was discharged to a foster-home. She was then transferred to another and yet to another and to a third one in a matter of a little over a year. Such transfers were not due to her behaviors.

Everything in D's life seemed to happen as an uncanny repetition of abandonments and lack of understanding, almost exactly as if she had been a toy, a doll, passed from hand to hand, fought over, but just as certainly dropped somewhere only to be picked up again later. Her story also powerfully tells about the appalling lack of knowledge or of intelligent delegation of the people who made such repetitions happen over and over again. The evaluation was politely filed away and disregarded.

I also have seen a few of children such as D, whose life seemed to be repeated even in the way people in charge of their treatment behave and I have felt this odd pull myself, certainly reminiscent of the projective-identification mechanism. Without the power of a knowledge or at least a critical eye on oneself, such pull is indeed likely to bend someone's perception and actions in a particular, surreptitiously determined direction and to confirm and perpetuate the child's self-fulfilling prophecy.

Who's the Man Now?

R was born the only child of an unmarried couple, who had been in a relationship for a few years but separated when R was a very young child.

Pregnancy and birth were unremarkable aside from mild perinatal anoxia and R was reported to have been an easy infant, average in his activity and demands. R also met his developmental milestones within average range and his early childhood was negative for physical or psychological problems.

As R's biological father had had no involvement whatsoever with his son, his parental rights were terminated when R was about three years of age.

About a year later, R's mother married a man but this relationship ended in a divorce in 2001, due to physical abuse. Three years later R's mother met her current husband, whom she married in 2007. This man, his three sons from a previous marriage, R and his mother eventually moved in together in 2008.

There was no report of significant behavioral or psychological problems until R was in Elementary school, at which point he related that he was "called gay," "picked on" and had a few altercations. Some similar problems were mentioned when R was in Junior High.

At the beginning of his 9th grade, R reported having "got a girlfriend", with whom he had a social relationship without much sexual interest but soon felt rejected by her, as she did not acknowledge "officially" their relationship when with friends. Around October of 2008, he decided to "dump" her but also found that he was "drifting away" from a male friend, "really a brother" and from another male friend who "chose a girl over me."

R reported that he was a sort of counselor to his friends, advising them, sometimes talking them out of suicide, which he reported was how he got closer to his "girlfriend," or convincing his best friend to quit smoking.

However, R was himself periodically thinking about suicide and reported a few gestures, including "slitting my throat with a knife," which he might have tried to rehearse by cutting himself on the shoulder but which appears to have been more theatrical than dangerous as no blood seems to have been shed.

At about the same time, R reported having experimented with various drugs (e.g. cocaine), possibly in an attempt at bettering or altering his psychological state but did not pursue as he was having "hallucinations", thus displaying another aspect of his ambivalence (i.e. doing/not doing.) R also began to go to school wearing a suit, a tie and a briefcase.

In November 2008, R was admitted to a local psychiatric hospital, following threats of suicide made to friends over the phone. R was discharged by the end of the month and began receiving outpatient psychiatric and counseling services.

Mid January, however, R wrote a note threatening to kill two peers (i.e. the male friend who had "betrayed" him and his girlfriend) and exhibited to his best friend the loaded .25 caliber gun he had in his jacket.

Paranoid formation of mild intensity.

Such formations are very often the result of a conflict revolving around issues of homosexuality and/or gender identity, which predisposes to feelings of vulnerability and primary femininity in boys and men.

This is to be distinguished from paranoia, which is a severe psychotic disorder deriving from similar conflicts but drastically multiplied by particularly harsh circumstances in very early childhood and/or by the expression of a genetic component.

Individuals with paranoid character, or in paranoid crisis, are typically hypersensitive to slights and blame, suspicious, mistrustful, overly jealous and vengeful.

They may function quite well alone but usually have significant difficulties with authority figures and jealously guard their independence. They are well-attuned to the motives of others and to the power structure of groups. They are also very precise scanners and will notice and focus on details more than they will perceive and process the larger picture (e.g. Rorschach.)

It is thought that R's very strong bond to a loving mother, without any significant competition and possible identification with a father-figure resulted in the development of homosexual and/or narcissistic fantasies in which he identifies with the feminine, "passive-receptive" pole, which the reported witnessing of a physically abusive relationship between his mother and one of her husbands, when R was between ages five and seven, might have crystallized.

As R began to participate in social interactions (i.e. Elementary school,) his apparently feminine presentation triggered negative feedback, which caused a series of extremely hurtful narcissistic injuries, mostly repressed at that young age but that re-appeared several years later as puberty inevitably brought up sexuality.

R then organized his defenses around denial, looking at sexuality as a neutral issue and around reaction-formation and projection, as his own unconscious fantasies at being a passive recipient of male power was expressed through its opposite: a radical rejection of authority figures and of the violence they reputedly impose on others.

On the other hand, the homosexual component was indirectly expressed through R's intense friendships with boys and his jealous retaliation against them (i.e. threatening to shoot the friend who "chose a girl over me") but never reached awareness as such.

As homosexuality, as well as mere homosexual fantasies, run deep against the grain of the dominant culture, social pressure and shame locked this dynamic into place, leaving little or no room at all for R to openly explore and test his fantasies and/or develop an identity thus creating explosive conditions.

After R broke up with his "girlfriend", with whom he had a purely platonic and token relationship, he found himself abandoned by his male friends, who each had actual girlfriends. Simultaneously, his mother had become a wife and a mother of four, leaving R in a less than central position.

The resulting feelings of isolation, envy and betrayal re-opened narcissistic wounds, which resulted in R increasing his defenses by over-compensating his passive-feminine fantasies and dressing up as the opposite: a powerful adult man in suit, tie and attaché-case.

This first acting out also suggested a strong exhibitionistic component, as if saying "Now you see that I am a powerful man." However, the exhibitionistic act requires that a strong effect be produced in the witness, which the exhibitionist uses as a temporarily reassuring proof that his masculinity is indeed there. One can surmise that past the initial surprise, R's appearance probably generated more derision than awe in the high school.

R's exhibitionism had to move up a notch up the symbolic scale, and he began to bring a loaded gun in the school. At first, the mere knowledge of having, on him, in violation of the rules of authority, this powerful, potentially lethal phallic symbol was enough, but the nature of the exhibitionistic dynamic required that there be witnesses to it.

At this juncture, it appears essential to note that none of the tests administered to R suggested the presence of a significant aggressive component. A case could be made that objective instruments (e.g. TSCC, FVAT, MMPI) are typically rather face-valid and that responses can be patterned to produce a desired impression. However, when a projective instrument like the Rorschach, devoid of any face-validity, agrees with all the other tests administered, the likelihood of an actual but undetected aggressive/violent component falls close to zero.

This aspect is also of interest as it significantly decreases the likelihood of violence against the self as well.

R's vacillations between the masculine-active and the feminine-passive poles are reflected in his symptomatic vacillations, also clearly evoked in the test results, between depression, anxiety and/or odd ideation and perceptual experiences (i.e. passive "mad") and angry, oppositional and defiant attitudes and behaviors (i.e. active "bad".)

On the whole, therefore, data from this evaluation described an adjustment disorder with disturbance of mood, emotions and conduct having reached the proportions of a paranoid decompensation in large part due to unconscious but very active conflicts around homosexuality and/or gender identity issues.

Prognosis is guarded at this time, therefore, due to the presence of the paranoid component, which refers to a relatively archaic dynamic and which might have begun to pervade aspects of R's personality, thus becoming increasingly ego-syntonic.

Psychotherapy, individual and/or group, should represent a modality of choice in this intelligent and verbal teenager, who appears curious about his actions and motivations. A relatively resilient psychological structure also increases the likelihood that R would not feel so overwhelmed by therapeutic work (i.e. transference, regression) as to decompensate while in treatment.

Data suggested the possibility of serious narcissistic injuries somewhere along the phallic and or Oedipal stages (i.e. age four to six) and, a little later, while R was targeted by peers at the beginning of his socialization in the school.

This last phase could represent a good entry-point into R's current dynamics and might even represent a bridge between R's current behaviors and symptoms and their historical roots.

R's transference is likely to be apparently passive, taking the form of superficial submission to the "power" and interpretations of his therapist and to the rules and regulations of the milieu. This will constitute R's strongest resistance as his therapist will probably hear more than once his complete agreement with what is being "imparted" on him. Therefore, in order to be effective, psychotherapy will have to gain access to the aggressive layer and to explore the ambivalent pleasure experienced by R in submitting while secretly rebelling.

Symmetrically, counter-transference is likely to oscillate between a sense of domination (e.g. hammering interpretations) and of powerlessness at R's passive resistance.

Another avenue would be to explore frankly and with benevolent neutrality R's sexuality and sexual fantasies, as broaching this aspect directly will almost certainly trigger an upsurge of emotionally loaded material, both conscious and unconscious.

Data collected from different sources suggested a relatively low level of risk of harm to others or to the self, and suggested that an exhibitionistic dynamic, rather than a physically explosive one, motivated R's behaviors.

On a residential level, it is recommended to normalize R's milieu (i.e. same-age peers, unlocked unit) and to systematically target his difficulties with responsibility, honesty and accountability.

Comment

An interesting case that provides some insight into the category of "school shootings" and into how homosexual feelings, thoughts or fantasies, unconscious or even semi-conscious, in boys often trigger extreme reactions. I personally suspect that a more or less distorted form of repressed homosexual fantasies are present in virtually any shootings, by adolescents or adults, including women.

In individuals who actually carry out the act by firing their weapon at people, or in the case of rapists, the reassurance drawn from others' reaction is not convincing or strong enough for the perpetrator and the act needs to be actually carried out to produce the desired effect. This requires a marked break with reality, which the preceding escalation/isolation phase and the planning of the action or the presence of a pervasive social estrangement (i.e. antisocial) facilitate.

Society at large, in spite of rather recent progress is still deeply homophobic, in large part due to the high level of religiosity in this country, which multiplies boys' anxiety about their masculinity and in some cases precipitates psychotic, always paranoid, decompensations. I remember a youth I had seen for an intake many years ago, who asked me about half and hour into the clinical interview if I was gay because I was showing "way too much interest in my (his) life."

Who's On Top?

This seventeen year old girl was admitted from a group-home setting after she physically assaulted a female staff and a female resident. Her mother separated from her biological father when she was about 6 months of age and the next two years were spent living in poverty, occasionally homeless until Family Services were involved and L was placed in foster-care and with relatives until her mother completed her case-plan. She spent her childhood in a poor household, living off her mother's Social security disability insurance, with a sickly but reportedly abusive step-father.

Behavioral problems erupted with puberty and L was placed with her grandmother. Behaviors did not abate and, at age 15, L even lived for a while with an older "boyfriend", a member of the armed forces. After having lost interest in the relationship, she moved back in with her grandmother and continued to display concerning behaviors, such as elopements, severe outbursts of anger, physical assaultiveness, self-destructive gestures, self-injury, substance abuse, sexual promiscuity and failing academic performance. This took place in spite of several interventions, such as placement in therapeutic foster-care or in more structured settings.

Data from this evaluation converged in suggesting a dominantly hysterical dynamic originating in disappointment by the parent of the same sex and over-stimulation by the opposite-sex parent.

Growing up in an environment where her stepfather was aggressively dominating, "strict" and occasionally violent to a passive, uninvolved or otherwise absent (i.e. drugs) mother, L is thought to have unconsciously admired her stepfather's power while superficially adopting her mother inhibited submissiveness.

It is also possible that L was over-stimulated in more explicit and manipulative ways, which would account for the intensity of her behaviors, for the partial amnesia she reported (i.e. up to about six) and for the presence of several "red flags" in the data.

An ambivalence can also be observed in L's shifting identification between victim and aggressor, particularly on females, as exhibited while at her previous placement in a group-home and since her admission here. It is also observable in her being fickle in relationships, for example losing interest in her older boyfriend "a couple of weeks " into the relationship.

Such dynamic hypothesis, placing L within the borderline level of organization of an emerging histrionic personality offers a better fit to the data and provides a simpler and more logical account of her signs, symptoms and behaviors than a manic-depressive dynamic.

An hysterical/histrionic dynamic would also explain the presence of guilt as L's unconscious identification with her abusive stepfather also results in her being assaultive to females, thus initiating a backlash of guilt afterwards. It is possible that L's two reported suicidal gestures might directly derive from such after-shock of guilt and such hypothesis should be kept in mind for future reference.

Since the hypothesis offered here assumes an hysterical dynamic, it is recommended that psychotherapy focus on L's relationship with her stepfather. Her current resistance is to present him as an overly abusive man, strong and mean who abused both her and her mother, thus warding him off as an object of desire. However, L has been sexually promiscuous with older males from a young age, thus clearly indicating sexual fantasies involving her stepfather, and the discrepancy between these two aspects could be used as an entry point into recollection of the first six years of her life, currently lost in amnesic fog.

Alternately, psychotherapy could explore the complementary perspective of L being repeatedly assaultive to females, and the rather evident connection between her behaviors and that of her stepfather towards her mother. The goal here would obviously be to bring closer to the surface identification to the stepfather and the underlying homosexual fantasies typical of hysterical dynamics.

Transference to the female psychotherapist is likely to reflect L's ambivalence between homosexual identification to the abusive father (i.e. imposing his power upon mother) and heterosexual identification with the abused mother (i.e. being dominated by the male). L's therapist could thus vacillate between feeling abusive or abused. Progressive interpretation of such counter-transferences could prove helpful to bring up L's transference and thus to help articulate her fantasies, thus altering her behaviors.

On a residential level, female staff is likely to experience similar vacillating feelings and it is recommended that they remain as neutral as possible in the face of L's verbal and emotional assaults, in effect looking at her like a demanding five year old girl and behaving accordingly, without, of course, being condescending. Remaining neutral with L (i.e. patience, slow rate of speech, low tone, relaxed attitude, firm speech) might prove very difficult but she is likely to grow from the feedback offered by a consistent, firm, unflinching and caring female. Interpretation should be left to the psychotherapist.

It is thought that alcohol and substance use are used by L to facilitate her shifting identification, to facilitate a form of semi-conscious dissociation that will allow her to play a role in a more convincing manner, to herself and to others. Such use would resemble that of exotic dancers who need substance in their system to perform convincingly. It is possible that sexual stimulation be used in a similar way, creating the condition for an addiction.

Family counseling is thought to be meaningless at this time and until L reaches a minimal understanding of her dynamics. In the mean time, contacts with the family should be maintained within a friendly, non-threatening and superficial framework. It appears evident in the view of L's history for the past few years that independent living has become the only viable option after L's discharge and it is recommended that this option be worked through and processed in absolute priority.

Comment

I chose to privilege the hysterical hypothesis over the borderline dynamic due to L's pervasively gendered behaviors. Which seemed to repeatedly, compulsively, refer to a triangle self/woman/man with very shifting identifications. I didn't see L's conduct only as the result of the stormy development of a bisexual identity because of the very large amount of anger she packed. This anger also seemed to be organized rather than merely impulsive, as spectacularly demonstrated by her self-injury. I remember seeing on her calf a perfectly square shape of methodically scraped skin. Although borderline do display episodes of violent anger and self-injury, these are typically impulsive and uncontrolled.

Both borderline and hysterical clinical pictures might evolve from an actual sexual abuse, which I suspected was the case with L. In fact, studies have suggested that up to 80% of women diagnosed with borderline personality disorder had been victims of sexual abuse as children.

There is also a large symptomatic overlap between the two but, of course, the conflicts and dynamics, as well as psychotherapy, are very different. Since hysteria has been thrown away with Freud, most hysterical people are now treated as if they were borderline and thus do not receive the correct approach to their problems. This was the case for L, who wound up in numerous Dialectical Behavioral Therapy groups with no benefit. On the contrary, I suspect that this was irritating to her as such groups were typically filled with girls.

Undiagnosed Asperger's

This fifteen-year old boy was admitted following out of control behaviors in the home, including violent outbursts, stealing, refusal to follow elementary rules, leaving supervision. Over the past year, these behaviors, in addition to occasional mild self-harming impulses and self-reported suicidal ideation, motivated several admissions to residential facilities for stabilization or treatment.

Development was remarkable for over-attachment to the mother, mild deficit in motor-skills while childhood was positive for very dysfunctional social interactions (i.e. "He never had a friend").

There were two or three significant father-figures and no reported traumatic history. Enuresis has been a constant throughout H's life, including at the time of admission and during his stay in residential.

Data from this evaluation converged in suggesting the hypothesis of best fit of an underlying psychiatric condition more severe than the obvious signs and symptoms might have suggested and belonging to the Autistic spectrum.

A differential diagnosis of psychotic disorder in its prodromal phase was considered but appeared less likely (i.e. infinitesimal prevalence rate, +/- 1/10,000), less grounded in evidence (e.g. no clear positive symptoms) and in historical data (e.g. presence of a form of estrangement in early childhood.)

Once called "Childhood Schizophrenia" and circumscribed to a single medical entity, "Autism" has been re-conceptualized over time as a spectrum with Autism at one end (i.e. complete social withdrawal, mental retardation, no language) and Asperger's disorder towards the other end (e.g. presence of language, normal or even high IQ, estrangement from social world.) This spectrum now also leaves room at its upper-end for atypical conditions that do not meet the full current criteria for an Asperger's disorder but still present with the hallmark of the disorder: severe difficulties engaging in spontaneous, intuitive, reciprocal and empathic exchanges with the world.

Research is in the process of testing several neurological and neuro-biological hypotheses about the Autistic spectrum (i.e. deficient "mirror-neurons" system) but there is still no agreement on the exact mechanism underlying this chronic disorder.

It is thought that H' entering adolescence, where relationships, including in their sexual aspect, are central to the development of an identity, has multiplied the impact of his social difficulties and has left him with no alternative other than explosive and regressive behaviors (e.g. over-attachment to mother.)

It also appears that, at least secondary to the many unpleasant consequences of these behaviors (e.g. removed from home, lack of freedom, loss of habits and routines) for about a year now, H developed a dysthymic component.

As studies have shown a prevalence of sleep problems in autistic and Asperger's individuals, this hypothesis might also account in part for H's refractory enuresis.

If the diagnosis offered here is correct, it designates as core treatment goal the development and /or acquisition of social skills, that will be learned, repeated and rehearsed until acquired on an intellectual level as logical connection between elements. In particular, any intervention or motivational intervention that would rely on "internal reward" is likely to be completely ineffective, while external reward systems, such as token economy, tend to me more successful.

Use of logic and rules (e.g. if A then B) rather than of emotion-laden constructs, such as moral judgments, empathic reasoning or metaphors should guide interactions with H. This might be more difficult to implement because we automatically and unconsciously tend to integrate our emotions into our communication and behaviors.

There is a large amount of resources available in the community and on the Internet, support-groups, forums and similar venues for parents but also for "Aspies" themselves.

Comment

This interpretation was completely ignored by all the individuals involved in H's treatment team and he was discharge after over 18 months with minimal or no change, aside from an increased eagerness to leave the facility.

This case highlighted for me the resistance against a diagnostic the prevalence of which however seems to have increased over the past several years. Psychiatrists do not like the diagnosis and I have never been able to establish exactly why. They seem to look at it as a neurological condition that they can't treat, preferring to target the signs and symptoms they have at hand with appropriate medications, which often include psycho-stimulants, anti-depressants or even anti-psychotics.

School people invariably look at high-functioning autistics as "faking it" and typically oppose a diagnosis that will force them to deploy extensive and/or specialized services around the child.

I believe that most of the progress accomplished by H during his inpatient stay was due to forced interactions on unit and to his participation to my group. In this setting, in which I insisted he be assigned, he initially remained silent but also intently listened to the other adolescents' banter, fight, flirt and exchanges. The group gave him the opportunity to learn social interactions and the members came to like his open, silent and smiling demeanor, which further reinforced his interest and motivation to learn. I made sure to encourage him to find the logic in the interactions, which he progressively did to the point that he was able after several months to occasionally participate verbally to the group and even to be respected and listened to by the others.

Another important aspect is the secondary development of a depressive aspect, which I observed in several high-functioning autistic boys since and which is very often masked by the clinician's assumption that a deficit in intuitive connection to the social world implies indifference to relationships. This is erroneous and Asperger's adolescents do suffer from their inability or difficulty in engaging others. Such loss often triggers a depressive dynamic and precipitates negative behaviors. An acknowledgment from the clinicians will go a long way toward consolidating the therapeutic relationship and initiating important progress.

Fifteen-Year Old Infant

This fifteen year old girl spent the first six years of her life in an erratic, if not chaotic, environment with heavy substance use, neglect and abuse, including sexual at the hands of parents and "friends" of the family. Eventually removed from this home with her numerous half-siblings, S was placed in foster-care and eventually adopted by the family at age eleven. Problems erupted at around age thirteen and escalated over the next couple of years. They included, apparently compulsive stealing, severe opposition, physical altercations and hoarding of food in her room leading to hygiene concerns and further conflicts.

Emergence of a personality structure derived from a traumatic early childhood. Such trauma seems to have been both cumulative, through early, regular exposure to a very dysfunctional and/or neglectful environment, and catastrophic, through instances of sexual abuse.

This traumatic history spanned several years, as S was about six years of age when she was eventually removed from her biological parents, which means that her early development was significantly disrupted and that the ways in which she adapted to her predicament became ingrained and ego-syntonic. In particular, it is thought that S evolved dissociative mechanisms that allow her to ward off intense feelings and emotions and to soothe her upset through a sense of control.

S's relationship to food appears to play a central role in such attempts and it is believed that she might use food as a symbolic vector for dissociative regression, which would explain why she apparently denies any issues in that area and why these issues have reached an explosive potential in her adoptive family.

S's history of seizure-like absences might also have been caused by an eruption of such dissociative episodes.

S's apparently compulsive stealing is thought to be also related to the same oral complex, as it translates into action a sense of "greed," an irresistible need of "having" what is wanted without delay. The fact that S's behaviors markedly degraded as she entered a different school in the much more stressful environment of Junior High, did support such hypothesis as her stealing would have acted as a regressive stress-reliever.

It is believed that when under the grip of such oral-aggressive states S actually dissociates, possibly hallucinates and regresses to the emotional state of an infant or of a very young child, which her history of neglect amply supports.

The dissociative defense would have been reinforced and further organized later, as S was sexually abused.

Sexually abused children typically develop dissociative mechanism as they have to maintain two separate sets of reality, the "child reality" with adults caring for them and the reality of the abuse, where the caring disappears and is in fact reversed as the child becomes a mere tool for the "caring" of the adult.

Diagnostically, S's clinical picture therefore appears depressive in nature, based on the symbolic very early loss of a reliable Mother-object and compensated by an oral-aggressive "taking-in" of the mother (e.g. food, other wanted objects) as a way of making her controllable and ward off the fear of annihilation. This is in keeping with S's focus on parts rather than wholes and with the schizoid aspect revealed by the Rorschach.

Prognosis is therefore guarded at this time since the pathogenic complex is very ancient, archaic in nature and heavily protected by dissociative, probably hard-wired, mechanisms. On a positive note, S's survival strategy seems to have in large part preserved the integrity of her psychological structure from psychotic fragmentation, which leaves some room for developing psychotherapeutic interventions.

As with all severe cases, conceptualization should optimally inspire the residential aspect of the treatment since no lasting change can be reached without repetition of nearly identical experiences. S is also one of the few cases where the patient actually needs and grows from the containing environment that most other children oppose and defy, as such an environment offers a symbolic equivalent to a stable and reliable mother. The problem therefore becomes the opposite of what it is for most other children as treatment is about emancipation rather than about compliance.

Very regular psychotherapy, "feeding," sessions should be scheduled, preferably shorter and more frequent (e.g. four times a week, at fifteen minutes per session.) Psychotherapist should be ready to on occasion merely sit in, offering the comfort of a relaxed and stable object. Content-wise, it is recommended to not hurry any topic and to let S free-associate, while favoring emotional expression and verbalization.

Memories associated with S's traumatic are likely out of reach on a verbal level, since they are also obscured by normal childhood amnesia, but are likely to surface as behaviors (e.g. tics) or feelings, kinesthetic or otherwise. In such cases, the therapist recognizing them as such and mere descriptive focusing would probably be efficient as it would amount to the symbolic organization of actual memory traces. The same applies to dissociative episodes, which could be neutrally explored and discussed.

Content-wise, a possible avenue of investigation would be S's attitude and behaviors in relation to food. Keeping in mind that such issues, as in most cases of eating disorders, are about control, no excessive pressure should be applied to bring up this content either. An evidently related content would be S's memories and/or thoughts and/or feelings and/or fantasies about her biological mother.

An indication that psychotherapy is progressing would be an increase in S's clinginess, possibly the appearance of concerns about the therapist's integrity (e.g. anxiety about therapist's health) and the emergence of more clear depressive affect. This would herald the turning point that S has ceased to be "her own mother inside of herself" and is ready to emancipate from her therapist and from the facility.

Family psychotherapy is not recommended at this time and until S has minimally processed her ambivalence about her mothers, the biological one and the adoptive one. Until then, family sessions would likely reinforce the problem, by unnecessarily stimulating established defensive patterns. S's adoptive mother has been caring for her consistently for the past nine years and, evidently, family sessions will have to wait for individual insights to develop.

Comment

This case illustrates how an almost standard clinical picture can hide a much deeper disturbance. It also poignantly evokes the resilience of children in the face of adversity and terrible history. Cases like S's always bring the thought of how a child with such history could possibly still be alive and reasonably functional.

This evaluation was an attempt at inspiring a treatment along the lines of Kleinian theory, or at the very least, of object-relations theorie(s), which are the only ones allowing a form of understanding of pathology rooted in the very early years or even months of development and therefore can inform targeted treatment interventions. These theories are on the brink of extinction in the USA, and virtually unknown in the residential treatment business because they require too much time to assimilate and a level of knowledge, in particular about development, that is well beyond standard training and education, including within the medical field.

There is also a substantial sociological risk at leaving un-addressed problems originating in very early childhood even with benign presentations, as these are the ones that are likely to produce catastrophic outcomes, including homicidal, later in life.

This case, as many others, also illustrates the insistence of insurance outfits that family therapy be pursued regardless of its clinical relevance or appropriateness. They fall short of ordering this modality, still somewhat held back by what is left of the respect due to clinicians' judgment but the administrative pressure is there, with the implicit idea that reimbursement is contingent upon provision of "complete" services. This is another example, and a very irritating one for the clinician, of the blind obedience to a statistical dogma, systematically missing the technical reality that probabilities say strictly nothing about any given individual case.

Occasionally forced to run family sessions when it is not indicated or even counter-productive, clinicians wind up with useless or even damaging "Jerry Springer" sessions that merely replay the problems, leaving everyone bitter, disheartened or even resigned, angry and the problems absolutely intact.

The usual consequence of such idiotic sessions is that the family blames the clinician for not having, somehow, through the use of mysterious means, transformed the child into what they expect. Significant work in individual psychotherapy, for the child but also for the parents, is an absolute requirement to fruitful work in family sessions and no one should be able to dictate or even suggest a modality that the clinician decided not to use.

No one in his right mind would question one's surgeon's decisions or one's pilot in command actions. The same should for psychotherapy, particularly when the Patient has been admitted to an acute care facility.

Payback

Thirteen-year old girl admitted from a short-term placement where she had been sent following repeated elopements and apparently intractable cannabis use. She was brought in by her parents, mother and stepfather with whom she seemed to have a reasonably loving relationship.

Data from this evaluation converged in suggesting the presence of a dysthymic disorder originating in the losses incurred by A when she was about eight years of age. Specifically, A lost in a matter of days, all of her siblings who had been dotting on her since her youngest age, her father, who was arrested and soon after stripped of his parental rights, following a plea bargain on his sexual abuse of his own thirteen year old daughter and her mother, who spent the next eighteen months in jail for neglect and methamphetamine use and trafficking.

A also moved several time between placements over the next couple of years and lost her grandmother, who died during that time. The particular circumstances of these losses, especially A's father molestation and the drug use of both of her parents prior to the implosion of the family unit, prevented A's regression to an earlier developmental stage and left her with no other alternative than denial and suppression.

A's case appears typical of what is known as the "masked depression" underlying conduct problems in children and adolescents.

Objective, self-report instruments like the MACI allow for a large measure of control over the results, while projective tests like the HTP or the Rorschach are largely impossible to penetrate, which often results in the objective instrument reflecting the individual's conscious or semi-conscious attitude(s) and his/her mode(s) of defense, while the projective test typically invokes and evokes actual dynamics.

In A's case, one could clearly see her attempts at denial and suppression in her MACI profile, which described a cold, calculating and self-centered individual, while the HTP evidently depicted a depressed, helpless and withdrawn individual, thus resulting in a clear and therapeutically helpful clinical picture.

A's very successful attempts at denial were also supported by her theory about her predicament (i.e. "I am here because I voluntarily made poor choices") but opened on a more subtle level of interpretation as it therefore appears that A is expressing large amount of repressed anger at her mother through her behavioral acting out, up to and including her placement at this facility (i.e. the "prison" for "potheads"). In effect, A is stating "I do exactly what you did and now you know how I felt", fairly obvious hypothesis which is also supported by A's puzzling habit of routinely disclosing her intentions prior to acting out.

Finally, it is thought, and supported by a few data, that A's real sexual concerns are kept secret or bottled up in large part because they are unconsciously linked to her father, who sexually acted out on her sister and, more generally, to the "power of sex", of which she also became an ambivalent carrier as she reached puberty.

Processing of this aspect would require processing of A's relationship with her father, which is currently heavily defended, in part out of shame but also out of intense jealousy at having been "betrayed" and anger at having been abandoned.

Prognosis is deemed fair due to A's apparently resilient psychological structure, itself due to a relatively stable early upbringing (i.e. infancy to latency). Rapid and marked improvement should be observed as soon as psychological issues have begun to emerge and are verbalized. However, behavioral control and practice of reasonable behavior and communication with the parents will most probably be necessary for a few years after discharge.

Comment

This case illustrates a common strategy used by children whose parents have somehow symbolically abandoned them, after providing acceptable early years. At puberty, when an increasing amount of self-governance is expected form them, these children typically engage in a form of retaliation against the parent. As the targeted parents are also almost always aware of their lapse or disappearance, they experience guilt, which the child uses to further her vengeful agenda. As in A's case, nearly everything they do, the troubles they get into, amount to rubbing the parent's nose into it, as much and as hard as they possibly can.

It is also at the same time a form of regression, an objective refusal to take over responsibility of oneself and therefore an implicit request to be "taken care of", by which they unconsciously and subtly offer the parents an opportunity to redeem themselves.

I noticed that such a retaliatory, regressive aspect very often underlies elopements, particularly when they seem to be somewhat compulsive, lack in clear benefits or, of course, do not represent an effort at leaving an abusive situation.

I remember another adolescent, a seventeen-year old boy, who had been admitted specifically due to that type of behaviors. He had eloped repeatedly, for up to a week at the time, had fled the Police, evaded tasers but always kept his cell phone on him and called his mother occasionally with nearly sadistic refinement.

Eight Ball

This fourteen year old "black and Jewish" girl, according to her own description, was admitted following about a year of behavioral difficulties, self-injury, suicidal statements and substance use. Very intelligent, most probably significantly above average and with superior language skills and verbal reasoning abilities, this girl had spent the first years of her life with a mother who was essentially a prostitute and a drug user. Her father was in jail and was a "gang-banger".

There were two suicidal gestures, both through ingestion of "random" pills and both ending with Q "throwing up twenty minutes later". The circumstances of such gestures, at a friend's house or in the school, left little chance of success. Other symptoms included reportedly "stress-induced" alopecia that had developed over the past 6 months prior to her admission, disturbed sleep with recurrent nightmares about "violence" and compulsive features in relation to food.

Q's mother reportedly abandoned her several times, including in infancy, while also staying relatively present in her life. As an example, when Q's father, with whom she was living in Ohio, was sent to jail and twelve-month-old Q was left with a "girlfriend", her mother went to pick her up and brought her to another State, where great-grandmother was residing. A few months later, however, Q's mother went away, and came back a couple of years later. In Q's mother's words, related by great-grandmother, "I can't face things. I run away."

It appears that Q has lived for several years, possibly between the ages of four or five and about nine, with her mother and a stepfather, the father of Q's younger brother. This period ended as the couple separated and Q's mother abruptly disappeared shortly thereafter, leaving the four children in a motel room. Q remembers scenes of domestic violence between her mother and her stepfather, which she had nightmares about for a "long time."

After a temporary placement with an aunt in Nevada and California, Q was returned to her great-grandmother, probably in 2004. Available documentation covering the next few years is rather confusing, possibly reflecting Q's erratic moves between relatives and foster-care placements, but, due to oppositional-defiance and great-grandmother becoming overwhelmed by all the children she had to supervise, foster-care placements began to dominate.

All the while, it is unknown what were Q's mother's whereabouts but it appears that she did continue to occasionally keep in touch.

Data from this evaluation converged in suggesting the presence of a very long-term depressive dynamic with a strong oral component. This form of depression is known as "anaclitic", from the Greek to "lean on", as simply and clearly illustrated by Q in her HTP and develops from the loss of the mother, either symbolically (e.g. drug use, unavailability) or in reality (e.g. death).

When the symbolic loss takes place very early, before the end of the first year of life, at a time where the "mother-object" is not yet fully formed as a single entity, only fragments can be internalized while others are fantasized to be still available, thus giving rise to manic denial, to more severe disturbances (e.g. identification, splitting, paranoid projection, somatization) and to impulsive behaviors.

The internalization also incorporates the punishment for being responsible for the loss, which translates into self-deprecation and, later, into the sacrifice of one's pleasure in an effort to earn the affection of others.

Interestingly, considering Q's above average verbal abilities, this type of depression originates at an age where verbal abilities are not developed, which suggests that Q might attempt to atone for being "bad" by being "smart", and has been able to sublimate part of her oral strivings into a verbal (i.e. still oral) mode, which possibly represents an asset for treatment.

The pathological complex, however, is largely pre-verbal and inaccessible by intelligence and verbal processing alone, which will require particular attention in psychotherapy and, more generally, in communicating with Q. Most of this complex will be only accessible "relationally" through the unconscious transference that Q is very likely to project on her caretakers, her psychotherapist but also others.

All sorts of orally-based signs, symptoms or behaviors (e.g. digestive tracts problems, eating disorder symptoms, addictive, immediate need fulfillment) are possible, along with alternating greedy neediness for and rejection of caretakers.

In her oral dependent and aggressive vacillations, Q is also likely to use her verbal abilities as a symbolic way of attacking, demeaning and dominating others.

Therefore, in spite of her apparent sophistication and of her above average intelligence, Q's current depressive state is thought to be based on a very archaic dynamic and a good indicator of her progress would be her ability to develop a more advanced depressive position, based on genuine grief and anger at a realistic image of her mother.

Although probable early exposure to sexual activity (i.e. mother prostituting self), or even actual molestation, evidently contribute to Q's ambivalent identification with her mother, earlier conflicts and traumas, as suggested above, are thought to dominate Q's current dynamics, but might also emerge as/if treatment progresses.

Prognosis is therefore guarded at this time and improvement will be dependent upon whether or not psychotherapy will be able to access the root of the problem. However, temporary, superficial improvement (i.e. re-adjustment) is also probable and might be enough to allow Q to weather the mid-adolescence crisis that brought her to treatment even if further problems are likely to emerge later in her life.

It is thought that treatment will be more productive if a first phase focuses on providing Q with systematic opportunities to develop a stronger sense of the stability of the "mother" through the stability of her primary caretaker(s). These important figures should be limited in number (i.e. psychotherapist, primary staff) and a fixed routine of "care-giving" could be organized, for example with very regular check-ins, at fixed days and hours.

The content of the interactions between Q and these figures is of much less importance than the ability of such figures to tolerate her oscillations between neediness and rejection, offering consistent, neutral and benevolent but reality-based responses. Very close cooperation between the caretakers is seen as essential as a stable image can only emerge from close similarity and consistency. Interactions with other staff can proceed without modification.

In psychotherapy, during this first phase, Q is likely to use her intelligence and mostly her verbal strength to ward off strong emotions and it is suspected that such display of intelligence is in fact a symbolic act of aggression, a projection of a "bad" part into the therapist. The therapist might feel inferior, "taken for a ride" and possibly angry.

Identifying and reducing this resistance will most probably constitute the main task of psychotherapy during Q's stay, with the goal of fostering the flow of suppressed or denied emotions and of minimally articulating them into coherent, reality-based narratives.

It is thought that such interpretive and constructive work should take place only if/when Q's resistance has abated, when genuine emotions have begun to flow, failing which Q will use it to buttress her resistance, which might even quickly lead to a stalemate.

Other interventions could be devised or existing implementations revised or adjusted through regular cooperation and sustained exchanges between residential and clinical personnel.

Comment

Q was very aware of racism but I have never met anyone who genuinely looked at race issues with such matter of fact, almost indifferent attitude. She also claimed her Jewish identity, which had been rigidly enforced by her staunchly religious great-grandmother.

Q's indifference even had an antisocial flavor, as if nothing really mattered aside from the satisfaction of her own needs. And indeed, her early life-history could have created the conditions for the development of such personality. But I don't believe this was the case for Q, mostly due to the many signs and barely disclosed symptoms of her very real suffering.

She was a very endearing young lady with a strong sense of humor, the "politeness of despair" as an English writer put it. She was also extremely headstrong, negating reality if need be, and her clinical picture was a hodge-podge of mild signs and symptoms, while her pain was actively and subtly denied, another example of superficially benign presentation.

Her insistence to wear a wig, purportedly to hide her alopecia was also suspicious as her hair loss was very light and hardly visible. The wig seemed to symbolize and solidify what has been called an "as if" personality.

I would not be surprised if Q would evolve into a highly successful individual, carrying along her silent World of suffering and, some day, "out of nowhere", decompensate into a severe presentation.

Borderline Pride

Twelve-year old at admission K was referred after a year of increasingly oppositional behavior and instances of physical assaults mostly in the school but also in the home. Middle child of three siblings, K was born asphyxiated and required three days of oxygen therapy before being surcharged to his family. Developmental milestones were reportedly met within normal limits although K's mother was not very specific in her report. Problems started at the beginning of second grade and steadily worsened over the year. In the third grade, K had fallen behind his peers and started to be teased. Behaviors further escalated and K was eventually placed in Special Education at around age 10, about three years after the onset of his behaviors. However, this did little to improve his behaviors and the year before his admission, K had had over 50 days of absences and 15 disciplinary reports.

Cognitive evaluations available at admission gave an overall level of intelligence slightly below the lower end of the average range, with even lower scores in the auditory memory realm.

Results from this evaluation suggested the presence of a dysthymic dynamic with increased irritability and strong compensatory, phallic acting out and fantasies. The original loss is thought to have taken place through the very painful narcissistic injury received when K realized that his intellectual abilities were not on par with that of his same-age peers.

Over-protected before school-age, perhaps due to his difficult birth and the possible focal organic damage caused by serious anoxia, K was soon confronted to a world where his belief about himself, as derived from his mother's unconditional and possibly compensatory admiration (i.e. PACI) met the hard wall of his intellectual limitations.

Indeed, test results from the past couple of years converged in suggesting a true overall cognitive level somewhere between the upper end of the Borderline Range (i.e. 80-84) and the lower end of the Low Average Range (i.e. 85-89,) although these estimates might derive from a clear deficit in short-term auditory memory, thus repeatedly under-estimating K's intelligence level (e.g. performance in mathematics).

K's many references to weapons, shootings, various phallic objects as well as his occasional resort to physical violence appear as compensations for the endured humiliation of having less "power", of being somehow deficient, of having been somehow "castrated".

Nowhere more than in the school environment is such a predicament more obvious, which explains why K's difficulties have taken place, and take place, in the school or in relation to the school. A concerning aspect of the data was K's tendency to isolate from his peers and possibly from his family as well (i.e. HTP,) possibly marking a drift toward unrealistic, possibly paranoid, self-reliance and over-emphasis on fantasies, thus creating the conditions for violent acting-out.

Prognosis is therefore guarded at this time and as long as K's drift away from the social world is not interrupted and a realistic sense of achievement and self-worth is not integrated and consolidated.

In the view of the above, it appears both logical and necessary to rapidly and significantly alter K's course in the school environment. To that end, it then appears inevitable to design and implement a system of aides, which would help K overcome his short-term auditory memory deficit, thus freeing the potential of his other abilities (e.g. written vs. oral instructions.) Each progress should be emphasized and capitalized upon, with the goal of creating a dynamic of success, which would most likely prove to be the most powerful therapeutic tool.

In individual psychotherapy, focus should be placed on K's sense of humiliation and loss, which he might not be able to verbalized at first. Aggression and phallic compensation should be progressively interpreted as attempts at preserving a sense of self-worth in the face of the painful sense of inferiority. It is possible that family issues, particularly relationship with father, might appear meaningful in this context.

The nature of K's deficit could be examined with him and discussed openly, which, in itself, could also bring a measure of relief. Of course, such work should be initiated with K's mother and progressively brought up in family session.

Comment

This case illustrates a problem I have encountered several times over the years, where psychological and behavioral issues derive from the child's hurt pride at knowing he/she is cognitively slow compared to peers. This always takes place when the cognitive functioning falls within what is called the "borderline" range, spreading between the low average and the upper end of the mental retardation range, with an IQ somewhere between the low seventies and the high eighties.

These children are constantly submitted to the well-meaning but hypocritical message that they are "like the others" while realizing that they are not. Feedback from some peers further irritates their narcissistic wound and the only pride-saving strategies available to them are to over-compensate with violent fantasies and/or with acting-out or to withdraw.

I always thought that acknowledging and clearly defining with these children their limitations, rather than to pretend that there were none was the only productive clinical way to help them adapt to their situation.

In K's case, mother's denial and over-protection made things worse and implicitly validated K's logical conclusion that the social world was a place to avoid, fostered a form of estrangement that even mimicked psychotic drift, while frustrating a need of interactions that grew as he reached pre-adolescence and consolidated a depressive dynamic.

I also suspect that mother's denial masked actual developmental signs or delays that could have alerted professionals and triggered early interventions.

Phallic Pride

Tall thirteen-year old admitted following predation of his nine year old brother through sodomy over a period of a few months. The family lived on a large ranch and S's father was absorbed with long hours and wide responsibilities. As the mother was also working in a nearby town, the children were left alone after school and until the evening.

S was reported to have reacted strongly to the birth of his brother and to have reverted to encopretic behaviors at that time, often defecating on the floor. After a period of stabilization, S resumed oppositional and encopretic behaviors from around age seven to eleven, at a time where he reported having had increasingly sexual thoughts.

Over this period of time, he was also reported by his mother to have been generally mean to others, manipulative, roaming the house at night and generally "bossy". He also tended to withdraw from the social world and surfed the Internet in search of pornographic material.

However, in spite of a lowering of his achievement scores over the end of this period, reports from school were all positive and described S as a good, helpful and enjoyable student.

He half-coaxed, half-coerced his younger brother to be sodomized and the situation ended when the mother eventually walked in the children.

S' clinical picture presented with a complex differential diagnosis and data from this evaluation first allowed to rule out two initial concerns.

The apparent lack of contact with reality suggested by S's perpetration, his apparent estrangement from the social world and reports of possible positive symptoms did suggest the possibility of a psychotic disorder in its prodromal phase. However, S's profile on the Rorschach, the best available instrument to tease out psychotic processes, was clearly negative for this kind of pathology, as the typical perceptual and cognitive distortions were not observed.

The scales tapping an autistic dynamic yielded discrepant results but, overall, the likelihood of an Asperger's disorder appeared very low as S's apparent estrangement from the social world presented a degree of variability very inconsistent with the pervasiveness of autistic features. In other words, S did appear to live in a fortress, but not in an "empty fortress".

Finally, historical data did not contain any element or suspicion that would allow to hypothesize an early sexual abuse.

On the whole, data from this evaluation converged in suggesting the presence of a severe case of developmental arrest at the phallic-narcissistic stage.

Starting at the earliest at about age two, boys transition from the pleasure and empowerment obtained through anal activity to a phase where the phallus becomes the primary erogenous zone. This phase is still essentially narcissistic (i.e. self-centered) and children are therefore relatively indifferent to others, as their grasp of object-relations is not fully developed as yet. Boys that age often exhibit themselves, are fascinated by their erection as well as by phallic symbols such as knives, guns, big cars, trucks, planes etc.

In S's case, this phase coincided with the pregnancy of his mother with his younger brother, which initially triggered a regression to the anal stage, the last successfully completed stage, with S becoming systematically defiant and displaying encopretic behaviors.

It is thought that the circumstances through which this crisis was negotiated by S' parents (e.g. physical punishment? withdrawal of emotional availability?) resulted in a sense of symbolic castration and ensuing humiliated rage, which expressed itself through a number of negative behaviors but increasingly through a general emotional "lock down," as if S had resolved to "keep everything in" from that point onward. Which is thought to be also reflected in his stuttering, as if refusing to let words out and, similarly, in his refusal of sustained eye-contact.

Under the surface and now mostly unconsciously, the original conflict remained very active and took an increasingly, compensatory, phallic aspect at S grew, to culminate with the phallic "possession" of his younger brother. As there was no sign of homosexual or pedophilic fixation or interest, S's acting-out logically appears as such a powerful, unresolved, not object-oriented, phallic-narcissistic, masturbation-like, reassuring repetition.

On the other hand, S appears to be very disturbed by his actions but cannot verbalize his emotions as they are still under the "lock-down" law and as they are the product of a mind partially fixated at the developmental level of a four-year old.

There is undoubtedly a significant secondary dysthymic component as the consequences of S's withdrawal from the pleasures and rewards of an active social life are inaccessible to him and as the symbolic loss of his mother has not been processed.

Prognosis is guarded at this time but will likely improve to fair, due to a resilient psychological structure apparently devoid of any severe anti-social, manic or psychotic features.

Family and individual psychotherapy should begin by focusing on the original problem and on the conflict(s) and relationship between S and his mother at around the time of S' brother's birth. S' memory is probably rather spotty but his mother's is likely to be more precise. It is thought that S harbors extremely high levels of unconscious or semi-conscious anger at his mother and that verbalizing such anger would go along way towards bringing up pathogenic material.

Individually, S' sexual fantasies and phallic preoccupation should be examined in details, with the goal of reaching the understanding that they are not object-oriented but narcissistic in nature and therefore significantly below the level of an average thirteen year old. An increase in such awareness would most probably facilitate the development of age-appropriate object-relations and help S loosen up his social isolation.

As S' defenses are organized on an anal-retentive mode (e.g. negation, denial, passive-aggressive, stubbornness) the same patience and persistence used during "potty-training wars" will have to be applied in session and S' psychotherapist will probably experience high levels of frustration, similar to what his mother experienced originally.

As S' defenses get looser, the depressive layer is likely to reach the surface and very large amounts of guilt and pent up emotions are likely to gush out, which will constitute a paradoxically positive indicator.

Comment

Looking back at this evaluation, I realized that the father, although present in the home, was totally absent from it, which reflects my own unconscious statement of his absence from his son's life as well. Indeed, a form of such absence is part of my own history and it is always amazing to me to see how unresolved bits of our history surreptitiously creep up in our clinical work, which is, or was, notorious in psychotherapy but much less so in evaluations.

When boys going through their phallic or Oedipal stage are not somehow uplifted by their father, or worse, when they are ignored or submitted to his disproportionate power, compensatory constructs are invariably built and always generate psychological, behavioral and sometimes personality problems later in life.

In this case, I am suspecting that S's estrangement was also a way of imitating what he saw in his father, who did everything on his own, in the "Cowboy way". It is also striking to see the extent to which this otherwise tall, handsome, intelligent and caring young adolescent was thinking and acting at the level of a four-year old in complete violation of reality, to the point that a psychotic or autistic estrangement could even be suspected.

Finally, the choice of sodomy, over other forms of sexual gratification such as masturbation or oral sex, betrayed the presence of regressed anal issues and of phallic aggression and domination.

Baby Bottle

Fifteen-year old girl who was admitted from a juvenile detention facility after two suicidal gestures. Daughter of a sixteen-year old mother who spent the first few years of her life cared for by her teenage mother and her grandmother.

After this peaceful period, I's mother married a man who turned out to be physically abusive while his son, a teenager at the time, sexually abused, in fact raped, I. This led to an immediate separation and divorce and to mother and daughter moving back in with the grandmother. Another relationship followed, abusive as well and negative behaviors began to appear in eleven year-old I in the form of substance use, defiance and promiscuity. Substance use escalated over the next years and became so systematic and refractory to any intervention that I was sent to juvenile detention.

Data from this evaluation, including I's presenting drug and alcohol dependence, converged in suggesting the presence of an emerging oral-dependent character structure, rooted in a dyadic bond to a very young mother, possibly with dependent traits herself.

At a very primitive level, such bond replicates the feeding situation, with the infant locked on the mother's breast and taking in the substance that makes her feel full and content, a primal fantasy that one typically sees underlying alcoholism or other systematic use of oral drugs. And the unconscious fantasy that probably also underlain I's suicidal gesture (i.e. drinking drain opener.)

As the males in I's mother's life have been unable to provide the stability they both needed, and have also been abusive, emotionally, physically and sexually, I has not been able to develop a sense of her own femininity through competition with her mother and remains at a very basic level of identification to her.

The dyad that existed in infancy, and where I grew for the first two to three years of her life, while teenage mother and baby-daughter were living together, alone with grandmother, still exists in many respects and I's acting out is seen as an expression of her rage at her mother for betraying and breaking this bond with males.

It is thought that I enacted such rage by emulating her mother, hence her current promiscuity with older males, which also amounts to giving her "a taste of her own medicine," while simultaneously preserving the dyadic bond through oral behaviors (i.e. drinking) and reports of various physical ailments.

Considering that I's rape by her older step-brother when she was about four years old immediately resulted in the break up of the family and the reconstitution of the original dyad (i.e. Mother-I with grandmother,) it is even possible that by being sexually promiscuous with older males, I is repeating symbolically this original situation with the unconscious expectation of a similar outcome and a return to the original dyad.

Of concern is the fact that I's regressed conduct and addictive behaviors appear to have become a relatively stable way of feeling, thinking and acting, thus evolving from symptomatic formations to emerging personality traits. Such traits are notoriously difficult to alter because they are experienced as part of oneself (i.e. ego-syntonic), rather than alien and unpleasant (i.e. ego-dystonic) and often leave the individual feeling as a powerless spectator of external forces (e.g. "I can't help it, ") merely displeased at the negative consequences of her actions.

It is thought that as she entered adolescence, the increased pressure towards emancipation and the developmental challenge of forming an identity have increased I's sense of powerlessness (e.g. HTP/Person) and triggered a more intense regression, which has in turn led to an increase in oral-dependent acting-out.

An underlying depressive component is thought to be currently masked by I's emerging character structure and by her self-medicating substance and alcohol use.

Prognosis is seen as guarded at this time, since, as mentioned above, personality traits are typically resistant to change, but could improve to fair since I psychological structure is still relatively malleable.

It therefore appears that family psychotherapy with I's mother would be an important initial component, with the goal of organizing a coherent narrative of mother and daughter early life and experiences, which would indirectly help a reality-based break-up of the fantasized dyad. The more details and the more reminiscing from either or both would be the better.

In individual psychotherapy as well, the central issue of emancipation versus dependency will likely be ever present, in content but also process-wise in the transference, and offers the best ground for progress. A depressive reaction is to be expected as/when I's dependency wanes, which would be taken as a positive indicator. The intensity of such depressive decompensation is difficult to predict but could reach concerning proportion, as orally-based depressions have a significant aggressive component. Close monitoring and prescription of anti-depressant could be indicated at that time.

On a residential level, and within the same perspective of facilitating emancipation and discouraging regression, a move from the locked unit, a symbolically holding, "mothering" unit, to an open unit, the age-appropriate unit is advised.

Comment

A mild example of substance and alcohol abuse as attempts to revive or re-experience an original dyadic bond between the child and the mother. I think this is the root of many addictions, which also explains why addictions tend to be so resistant to treatment. They are just as resistant and difficult to reach than any other pathology rooted in early childhood or infancy. The earlier the problem, the more severe the pathology and the more difficult the treatment.

Interestingly, such oral regression can use any substance or medium and I have met a few methamphetamine addicts who used to obtain a sense of fulfillment, calm and peaceful contentment which this very powerful stimulant curiously produced in them.

The most deadly of such oral addiction is of course that to heroin, which typically, and initially, provides a sort of Nirvana, an "oceanic feeling" that alludes to a complete, primordial merging with the "Mother" and is extremely difficult to abandon, in addition to the modifications in neuronal connection it quickly implements.

For all the adolescents I have met who suffered from a regression to this dyadic phase, there was invariably a history of very close bond with the mother without interference from or competition with another adult. In girls, this often triggers a pseudo-homosexual reaction and in boys a very intense sense of entitlement that can easily translate into criminal behaviors and a pseudo-antisocial presentation.

In the most severe cases, this bond was either erratic, switched on and off by an unstable mother or abruptly interrupted, the mother "disappearing", physically or emotionally, sometimes due to the use of substance and sometimes due to a depressive episode or to a combination thereof.

Another Round of Mothering

Thirteen-year old girl who was admitted following significant anger dyscontrol, recurring physical assaults against family members, hitting, kicking, throwing heavy objects and being generally out of control.

N was born from a brief relationship and her father was not aware of her existence until five or six years later, when N was placed in the custody of the State and admitted to a residential treatment facility for young children. N's mother's whereabouts where still unknown at the time of this evaluation.

As a result, very little is known of N's early childhood, except for what transpired during her almost two-year long residential treatment. In particular, an extensive history of sexual abuse was established and the likelihood of a chaotic early upbringing appeared extremely high.

N was discharged at around age 8 and placed with her father and his family, where she remained until admission.

Data suggested the central presence of a reactive attachment disorder of mild intensity, with mixed inhibited and dis-inhibited features, further complicated by the sequelae of repeated sexual abuses at an age where symbolic abilities are not fully developed.

Children with significant disruption in the development of emotionally trusting relationships remain fixated at a primitive level in their ability to experience, express and modulate emotions, to engage in relationships and therefore to learn through them. As a result, these children's experiences, including memories, tend to remain at the level of elementary perceptions, body-language, motoric output and behaviors, while the psychological defenses against the underlying conflicts (e.g. loyalty, ambivalence towards parents and adults) are archaic, often taking the form of denial and/or intense approach/avoidance.

Such perspective explains why it is very difficult for N to form close attachments to other people, why she avoids close friendships, appears indifferent, or appears to lack emotions. N will tend to superficially accept anyone as a caregiver, as though people were interchangeable, and will act as if the relationship had been intimate and life-long, while pulling away, at times violently, when the relationship threatens to become too real or too strong. Such extremely intense ambivalence is thought to sit at the core of N's conflict with her step-mother, which resulted in her placement at SJCH.

A reactive attachment dynamic accounts for other symptoms and behaviors more economically and more usefully than diagnoses of Oppositional Defiant Disorder or Attention-Deficit Disorders. The latter, in particular, appears more obviously dubious in the view of N's solid performance on achievement tests (i.e. Woodcock-Johnson) where she scored at or above her grade level.

N's sexual abuse constitutes a second, closely associated layer that reinforces some of the aspects evoked above, such as her approach/avoidance, while probably supplying most of the energy fueling her behaviors. Children who are over-stimulated at a young age, less than five-years old in N's case, tend to hard-wire a physiological base-line at a level higher than normal and, in effect, seek out the over-stimulation that will allow them, paradoxically, to return to a state of perceived calm. This dynamic underlie, for example, many of the "cutting" cases but also all sorts of hyperactive behaviors, anger-dyscontrol, so-called "mood swings," etc.

In addition, it is thought that, in part due to its pre-verbal origin, a significant part of N's sexual abuse has not been processed and therefore continues to feed her signs, symptoms and behaviors.

Prognosis is seen as guarded at this time, since most of the pathogenic material remains unconscious and is not verbally structured, but will improve in direct proportion of the work accomplished in that direction. The relatively mild level of N's disorder, in particular the absence of any psychotic indicator or of manic denial and N's intelligence and excellent verbal abilities constitute huge assets and significantly increase the likelihood of a successful outcome.

In individual psychotherapy, attachment issues will occupy center-stage, which will most probably be apparent in N's vacillations between negative and positive transferences and will also be felt in her counselor's counter-transference, through shifts between strong empathy and aggravation. It will be especially important for N's counselor to conceptualize her treatment as a continuum with an attachment phase, a growth phase and, most importantly, a termination phase. This course will have to be plotted with the utmost stability, including very regular appointment days and times, duration of sessions, and extreme care if/when absences or days off are scheduled.

Due to the high level of discomfort of most people, including counselors, with sexual issues, victims of sexual abuse are rarely helped through several aspects of their experience, particularly their physiological sensations and their interpretation of such sensations. This is further complicated in N's case by the very early age at which she was victimized and non-verbal expressions are likely to be more useful avenues. Rhythmic play (e.g. swings), doll play, putty, drawing, idiosyncrasies (e.g. hated food) will probably contain symbolic expressions of N's experience and it will be her counselor's work to notice, register, translate into words and to articulate such unconscious or semi-conscious "confessions", "small bites" into a coherent narrative. N's current sexuality, fears, desires and fantasies would also, of course, contain important material.

Work with N's biological father and stepmother in family therapy is recommended, with the goal of empowering them with effective parenting techniques and of encouraging them in their learning of N's reactive attachment disorder. N's counselor could fruitfully share with N's stepmother her own shifting emotional reactions to N's transference.

On a residential level, it is recommended to focus on building a solid relationship with a unit staff and to work on the separation as soon as this bond is established. The operational and psychotherapeutic part of the residential treatment will be the *emancipation* process more than the bonding or the "re-parenting" process.

Comment

N's stay and treatment in the facility where she was admitted after she was taken away from her dysfunctional mother and remained for over eighteen months probably saved her life. This facility in effect re-parented N and would have been a more effective placement this second time as well.

Recommendations issued here were not followed and N stayed about a year, during which she essentially learned to miss her family.

I would venture that probably about half of the hundreds of children I came across during my long tenure in a residential treatment facility improved due to the mere fact of being away from their family and in a structured environment. A placebo effect multiplied by the exposure to a suddenly broadened world.

The Pixie who Went through Hell

Nine-year old girl, thin, of short stature, L was admitted following acting out behaviors in her foster-care placement and in the school. Behaviors ranged from hurting the home's handicapped pet, constant lying, flooding toilets in the school.

L was born the healthiest of a pair of fraternal twins. L's sister suffered from a variety of handicap of mild severity in the sensory and cognitive realms. Her family also lived in poverty and her mother seemed to have an unconscious attraction to men with pedophilic tendencies. Including L's biological father.

L was instructed from an early age to not disclose to anyone the family's many problems

Data from this evaluation converged in suggesting a clinical picture dominated by the sequelae of several instances of sexual abuse and complex and erratic family dynamics. Ongoing, very tight and most probably threatening instructions issued by L's caretakers to deny the events of various nature, endured or witnessed, pertaining to the abuse(s) but also to the general state of poverty and dysfunction of L's family, have fostered the development of a dissociative-like state reinforcing the typical tendency seen in victims of abuse.

Such dissociation develops as the only way of living in two completely different realities, the abusive one and the "business as usual" one, the internal one and the external one, both intensely experienced by the child.

A rather striking manifestation of this double-reality was L's pattern of both Under- and Hyper-Response on the TSCC. It was also powerfully communicated by L's spontaneous drawings, which really appeared as an urgent, non-verbal disclosure and can be read in her compulsive lying (i.e. lying about the obvious is a way of saying "I am not telling the truth",) and in most of her behaviors (e.g. flooding the toilets in the school is making the "bad stuff" come out for everyone to see.) All being intelligent compromises between telling and hiding.

Another, typical, aspect of this duality was illustrated by L's pattern of approach-avoidance with psychologist and with the father-figures in her life. Approach-avoidance is a cognitive mechanism identified by social psychology that describes a response to a goal inspiring both desire and fear. As the individual approaches the goal, her desire diminishes and the fear increases and as the individuals moves away from her goal, the fear diminishes and the desire increases, thus perpetuating a sort of oscillation. Evidently, this mechanism is very frequent in victims of abuse, as the child both needs the closeness and the uplift of the adult, but fears the confusing and often hurtful ways in which the adult abuser provides this attention.

Another component of L's clinical picture is a very intense guilt, which is seen as having two distinct sources.

The first is thought to derive from a likely sexual abuse, as it realizes Oedipal childhood fantasies (e.g. being "grown up", having a "husband",) which thus seems to imply, from the child's perspective, a measure of responsibility in the abuse. This aspect is of course reinforced by the abuser as a sure way of securing the child's silence, by the aspects of the relationship experienced as positive by the child (e.g. closeness) and further deepened by the child's interpretation of her physiological response to the sexual stimulation.

This level of guilt can be observed in L's borderline compulsive way of going about a few activities (e.g. folding towel extremely neatly, cleaning) and to her very controlled and neat handwriting.

A second, and probably deeper, source of guilt is thought to derive from L's perception of her superiority compared to her twin-sister, whom she could have "harmed" in the womb and to her possibly being the most intelligent member of her family as a whole. This guilt is reality-based, mixed with shame and probably connected to a dysthymic dynamic. This aspect generates large amounts of unconscious ambivalence with anger towards mother and sister (e.g. hurt the disabled pet,) and also probably plays an important role in L's use or refusal to use (e.g. "dumbed-down" Wechsler) of her intelligence.

In that regard, it is noteworthy that L's intelligence also tends to increase her anxiety, as an intelligent brain works faster and better at creating more "realistic" meaning and at projecting scenarios into the future. This aspect, in addition to the hyper-alertness that inevitably develops in children living in an erratic, violent and/or abusive environment, is also thought to account for L's abnormal perceptual experiences, as discussed above in the Mental Status section.

A mixture of anxiety, hyper-alertness and guilt seems to account best for L's high energy-level and apparent inattentiveness and hyperactivity as her anxiety tells her that slowing down, expanding her focus and decreasing her motor output would most probably result in unacceptable thoughts, memories or guilty feelings to emerge or to gush out. Being hyper and superficial, rushing through her anxious world would be her way of "holding it in." A similar mechanism can be observed with many grieving individuals, who "keep themselves busy" out of the fear of being overwhelmed by their loss.

Prognosis is deemed to be fair due to L's intelligence, to the resilience suggested by the moderate intensity of her behaviors, to her ability to bond and to the dominant presence of anxiety in an overall mild clinical picture.

Verbalizing a few aspects of her traumatic life will most probably be enough to relieve L's stress enough that her behaviors will quickly stabilize at a level where the highest level of care will not be necessary.

L simultaneous need to disclose and to dissimulate translates into numerous symbolic disclosures, as evidenced by her spontaneous drawing when entering psychologist's office for the first time. Therefore, L is likely to send continuous little enigmas that she implicitly asks adults to solve in a game-like manner. Each of these small riddles will contain a piece of disclosure and it will be the therapist's work to translate it into words and to slowly weave the patchwork together in a coherent narrative.

Of particular note is the fact that the process of disclosure itself, or of mutually agreed upon interpretations, rather than any particular content, will be the primary psychotherapeutic element.

The deeper dysthymic aspect represented by L's aggressive/guilty relationship to her twin sister and to her mother is likely to be difficult to access. Following the hypothesis offered above that this complex largely contributes to L's under-use of her intelligence, it might be more fruitfully, albeit indirectly, tackled by stimulating and challenging L's intelligence through schoolwork, readings, games.

Relatedly, L is likely to hold back her academic performance at a certain minimal, acceptable level below her ability level. It is therapeutically helpful to progressively push her to express more of her potential. Tests data suggested that Mathematics, particularly pattern recognition and logical series, would be a first area of potential expansion.

Tests data also suggested that verbal conceptualization is a weakness, most probably for historical and psychological reasons. Again, it would be therapeutically helpful to foster the development of L's abstractive abilities over her tendency to revert to concrete thinking.

Interactions with her, such as responding to her questions or giving her instructions should always be a notch slower than her own rate of speech.

It is recommended to take advantage of the very few years left before L enters adolescence and its hormonal turmoil, to provide her with a firm and stable plan that would allow her to resume her emotional growth, possibly through some temporary regression, and to consolidate her accomplishments. Conversely, and although her clinical picture is seen as relatively mild, lack of permanency is likely to result, at least, in significant flare-ups.

Comment

Although an interesting case on a clinical level, L's problem clearly did not require a residential level of care. She was placed, like so many others, due to the lack of training and knowledge of the foster parents involved in her care, to the lack of training and knowledge of the vast majority of counselors available in the area and to the lack of knowledge and training of the State's workers and their supervisors.

On the other hand, as I mentioned earlier about another case, L spent a few months in comfort, with children her age, learned that there were adults with whom you could actually talk without having to meet any expectation. I also offered her the first raspberries and cherries of her life.

N's subtle strategy of telling a truth while lying in the face of the obvious was enlightening to me, as it opened a new avenue of understanding of why children lie, in addition to standard denial (i.e. criminal type) or regression to pre-object-constancy (i.e. not seen = doesn't exist). Their communication lies, so to speak, in the process, in the medium, and not in the content. It always refers to someone else, a parent, lying about important aspect of their life and presents a retaliatory, angry, aspect, which opens useful possibilities of investigation in psychotherapy.

Such investigation is all the more relevant since the accuracy with which children are able to discern that an adult is lying has been repeatedly demonstrated by experimental research, including recently with infant subjects. Their perception is highly likely to reflect a fact rather than a construction.

The psychotic-like symptoms alluded to in the summary were both auditory, whispers telling her to do "bad things" and visual, in the form of shadows seen from the corner of the eye or "flashes" of people being killed. I was not overly concerned that these symptoms were schizophrenic in nature for a number of reasons. Positive psychotic symptoms are exceedingly rare in children and, in my experience come with other problems such as a form of social estrangement or odd thinking. It is also important to remember that children have and keep for a long time the ability to bend reality to their will, which they use to play (e.g. "make believe") and to explore the World.

Little Atlas

This thirteen-year old boy was admitted after an outburst of rage during which he began to methodically destroy his home. W was born from an on-off relationship between a vagrant father, a "hobo", who disappeared for months or years at the time and a relatively stable but dotting and overwhelmed mother. W's father would reportedly stay for a few months, apparently rescued by W's mother, but was eventually "kicked out" and disappeared again. W stated that "he's like me. He snaps."

W's first behavioral problems appeared when he was about eight, in the school environment, where he was generally disobedient, occasionally defiant and explosive. This acting out in the school environment eventually led to a residential placement, which lasted for about a year. W was discharged back to his mother but soon reverted to the same pattern of acting-out in the school and this time in the home as well. He was re-admitted to the same facility and this is where and when this evaluation was carried out.

Data from this evaluation converged in suggesting the presence of a dysthymic disorder with early onset and of a mixed anaclitic (i.e. "needy",) introjective (i.e. self-loathing) type.

These depressed children have experienced a disruption in their relationship to a primary caregiver which is always perceived as a loss, real or symbolic. They experience feelings of helplessness, inadequacy, depletion, streaming from the internalization of the overly critical, punishing or demeaning yet loved/needed important other they have lost. They are readily upset by circumstances, easily overcome by their intense dysphoria and, once upset, have a very difficult time calming their feelings, which may linger as permanent sadness.

Living in such a state of emotional frailty, they often are very irritable, easily provoked into angry outbursts that are not easily overcome either and which are typically followed by waves of remorse and guilt. From their perspective, they are unsupported, misunderstood and even victimized, which they may occasionally defend against by resorting to the opposite: an attitude of arrogant entitlement.

In W's case, this dynamic is thought to have been brought about by a very ambivalent attachment to a violent and erratic father-figure and by the enormous responsibilities W endorsed very early on to be the only strong, stable and protective male in the family. Young children often attempt to tackle such a role when they realize that they do have a measure of power (e.g. about four to six years old), but in a normal environment abandon this fantasy to pursue their personal and social development with their peers.

In W's case, the stilted structure of his family environment, his mother and him, and possibly his mother's centering of her world around their dyad, made such development difficult or impossible. W's explosions thus seem to combine identification with a violent and unstable father, whose last name he carries, as a symbolic way of bringing him back to the family, anger at his mother for asking from him, if unconsciously, things he cannot provide, intense guilt and self-hatred at not being strong enough to provide those things (e.g. W's exceptional reaction to failure on the WISC), permeated by anxiety and by a deep sense of despair at the unfairness of his situation.

W's reported "black-outs" can be seen in this perspective as his attempts at suppressing these very thoughts as they threaten to emerge to his consciousness at the beginning of an explosion, thus at least neutralizing his guilt.

Another consequence of this regressed dynamic is that the normal process of emancipation, identity formation and advanced socialization, typical of W's age is thwarted, which adds to his sense of isolation, despair and unfairness as well as to his anger. As matter of fact, this dynamic even appears to block the academic unfolding of W's intelligence, in spite of a true IQ most probably set within the high-average range or even above (i.e. 110+.)

Within this dynamic context, it also appears possible that W's recent explosion might, at least in part, represent a successful attempt at leaving his home situation without experiencing the guilt of betrayal, while moving into a worry-free environment where he can be a child without any responsibility other than to follow instructions from people he does not care much about. There is also a striking parallel between W's leaving and coming back to his home and his father's errancies.

This state of affair, mixing helplessness, humiliated rage, guilt, hopelessness and identity moratorium becomes more concerning when seen in the perspective of W's impending pubertal changes. The influx of testosterone might significantly worsen W's subjective experience and his behaviors in the near future might show an escalation, particularly in their self-harming, self-retaliatory or even self-destructive aspect.

As W's explosions are thought to serve the purpose of suppressing and dissipating unacceptable thoughts about himself, his mother and his father, a logical goal of psychotherapy would be to investigate such thoughts. Reaching this content, resolving the "black-outs," will likely be a protracted process but would also achieve behavioral relief.

Reaching this content would also open avenues to processing deeper depressive layers, although W's is likely to refuse to engage into further psychotherapeutic process once the above goal are minimally met.

Until W reaches a minimal level of insight into his dynamics, family counseling is likely to be an irritant, or even a hindrance, rather than a helpful intervention. It is recommended that until such a point is reached, family sessions be maintained at a very superficial, "check-in", level.

If at all possible, although this does not seem very realistic, sessions with W's father, and/or with W's mother and father, would certainly be very helpful to W.

In the school, particular attention should be paid to both W's extreme vulnerability to failure and to his high-average level of intelligence. This creates a particular difficulty for school staff, since pushing W's limits appears necessary to improve both his self-regard and his academic performance, while also multiplying the risks of failure and therefore of humiliation and acting-out. It is recommended that every effort be made, however, to challenge W's intelligence.

On a residential level, no alterations to the standard model appear warranted at this time. It is however recommended that W's expectations not be influenced by his appearance of maturity and staff's attention is drawn to the fact that his true level of autonomy significantly lags behind what it appears to be. In fact, W might experience relief at being treated as a child, provided that his very fragile pride is respected.

Comment

During the administration of the IQ test, W failed the last item of a subtest and I helped him in a friendly manner to finish it, after the subtest was concluded. This was intended to neutralize his frustration, which I sensed, and thus to facilitate the following tasks, but was construed by W as the opposite: a demonstration of his inferiority for not having figured it out by himself. He became rigid, fists clenched, turned away from me and cried for several minutes. It was not possible to have him verbalize any emotions or thoughts about this event and the test had to be interrupted to preserve minimal validity. I resumed the administration a few days later and W showed improved focus and tolerance.

All the aspects of W's dynamics were folded within this very small and simple situation and it instantly became quite obvious why the school environment had given rise to W's initial outbursts of anger but also, how it would have been possible to assuage his felt humiliation very early on and to put his high intelligence on a productive, self-reinforcing track.

Instead of being the setting where W's frustration, sense of inferiority and enmeshment with his mother would be at least in part compensated, the school became the battleground where he could lash out without experiencing the guilt that paralyzed him at home. Until the testosterone upsurge of adolescence overflowed his defenses.

This case also provides a good example of how unresolved issues persist regardless of the measures taken to control behaviors. A year of residential treatment with standard cognitive-behavioral model, individual, group and family counseling returned W nearly intact to his mother and their unchanged conditions, so that the exact same behaviors re-appeared and worsened over the next couple of years.

Although the conditions in which a child lives often impede consolidation of the progress made in psychotherapy, I believe that behaviors, symptoms and signs will not return to a similar level or worsen if relevant interpretive work has been accomplished. Boosting the buck does not boost the bang.

Hurt in Infancy

B was born the only child of an unmarried couple in their late teens. Pregnancy was reportedly normal but birth was premature by about one month and by Cesarean section due to fetal distress. A cardio-vascular malformation had resulted in respiratory failure and anoxia and intensive medical intervention followed to keep the infant alive.

Once in her home, two to three weeks after her birth, B was described as a cuddly infant who was overly attached to her mother and appeared to suffer from separation anxiety, or rather panic, until about age seven or eight.

At about nine months of age, B's ankyloglossia (i.e. tongue-tied), a congenital anomaly, was surgically corrected.

Finally, B also had a minor malformation of her lower urinary tract that tended to generate infections and was surgically corrected when she was about eighteen months of age.

B's history was also remarkable for extreme temper tantrums, starting in infancy and extending to the present. These tantrums were described as very violent, lasting several hours and resistant to any intervention, including physical restraint.

B's mother identified a single element that occasionally seemed to help calm B down: her "security blanket", which she has since returning from the hospital, a few weeks after her birth.

According to her mother, these tantrums did not seem to have any identifiable theme, patterns, triggering factor or individual target.

B's biological father never was part of her life but two father-figures seem to have played an important role. The first one lived with B and her mother for about three years, returned when B was about eight and currently is B's step-

father. For about five years in between, another man lived with the family and fathered B six-years younger half-sister. According to her mother, B "got along" with these men, and keeps in touch with her half-sister father, whom she still calls "Dad."

Although B's mother described a relatively even course, with continuing behavioral explosions, across B's life, there seems to have been a first change when she was about eight years of age. At that time, almost "overnight", B seemed to become indifferent to her mother's absence, while she could not bear to loose sight of her mother before that. Her despair at not being in the presence of her mother appeared to turn to "anger at me."

It is also at that time (i.e. third grade) that B's mother separated from the father of B's half-sister and that B's grades were observed to plummet.

A second change was reported about two or three years ago, or when B entered the eight grade. From B's own report, she began to dislike "being around people", started to over-eat, to turn away from school work and to hang out with "stoners."

Her mother also noticed that when B was in a tantrum, she would now lock herself in her room, throw things around and come out a while later "as if nothing had ever happened."

B reported having been used as a sexual object by neighborhood older youth between the ages of five or six and seven or eight and on an occasional but also regular basis. This would happen when B was playing outside alone, which in itself raised questions in the view of her attachment to her mother and of her explosive temper. In addition, B did not report this situation to either of her parents and still refuses to process verbally the parts she acknowledges she remembers.

According to B, the abuse was successfully buried until she was in the eight grade and a friend of hers was raped. The friend confided in B who was sworn not to say anything but eventually let it "slip out" to the friend's sister. At about the same time, B's depressive drift, as described above, intensified and her behaviors (e.g. suicidal ideation, physical aggression) began to degrade to the point where a higher level of care became necessary.

B's suicide gesture/attempt was motivated by her "being tired of people" and performed through the ingestion of Trazodone, which "I can't sleep without." B reported having wanted to "sleep forever."

Clinical picture combining two aspects. The first and deeper layer involves a strong anxious component rooted in B's extensive early history of separation from her mother through multiple hospitalizations. As infants do not have the capacity to organize their experience through language and syntactically structured memories, their experience of such serious disruptions typically is overwhelming and often takes the proportions of an actual trauma.

In B's case such overwhelming, primitive anxiety became fixated on the availability of her mother and main caregiver, which translated into extremely acute separation anxiety and soon generalized through tantrums of panic-stricken proportions.

As B's grew and developed, she seemed to simultaneously evolve a counter-phobic defense, which consists in actively seeking the cause of her panic in an attempt at mastering it. In so doing, B also seems to have developed more efficient defense mechanisms that reinforced the denial of her separation from her mother, thus blocking her normal course along the separation/individuation developmental line.

As a result, sixteen-year old B is still in many respects an overwhelmed infant or toddler, one who has evolved powerful but archaic protective mechanisms such as dissociation, denial, splitting and projection.

In particular, through denial, B seems to have turned her painful dependency onto others (i.e. mother) into its opposite, the rejection of, and aggravation at "people." In such perspective, her suicidal gesture explicitly motivated by being "tired with people" would translate into a fantasized regression inside the Mother (i.e. "sleep for ever").

It also appears possible that B's efforts at coping with her reality by herself, in isolation and denial, would have contributed to her reported sexual abuse, as it would partly explain why a little girl terrorized when out of the sight of her mother could have wound up with abusive neighbors and could have let such situation last for several months and remain secret for several years.

From her first temper tantrum onward, B's anger, or rage, is seen as the behavioral expression of her primal anxiety and progressively developed in B a sense of being "bad", "damaged" or "crazy", which itself generated a dysthymic component adding a another ambivalent layer to her relation to "people" .

B's insomnia is seen as another expression of her anxiety.

As a result of her complex clinical picture, B's prognosis is guarded at this time. The archaic component being very organized and entrenched at the deepest level is seen as representing a potential danger, mostly to B herself, while her intelligence and relatively solid psychological structure represent strong assets. Metaphorically, one can look at B as a well-built house with a weakness in the foundation that has begun to affect the integrity of an otherwise resilient structure.

As B does have the means to process verbally, psychotherapy should broadly aim at coming to terms with her serious and pervasive attachment issues. The blueprint would be to resume B's separation/individuation development, the pre-requisite of which being her coming to terms with separation from her mother, and her symbolic "loss." A good indicator that this stage has been reached will be a depressive reaction, probably similar to the one B reported around eight grade. Of course, an increase in precautionary measures would be recommended at that time.

Anxiety should be part of this process but will likely present itself under a defended appearance. B's fascination for "serial killers", for example is thought to express such anxiety but through projection and denial. Her aggravation at "people", for another example, is seen as expressing through denial her anxiety at being deserted. As this process is unconscious, interpretation will require patience and tact and progress will likely be very slow.

Work on the sexual abuse will likely be helpful to loosen her current defensive structure and could also inform the above processes as it combines issues of dependency and isolation.

Family psychotherapy should also be useful, particularly if it examines B's mother own development in the early days or years of her motherhood, since she was very young at the time of B's birth, and if it involves cognitive and emotional anamnesis. This is seen as important as anxiety is readily transmitted back and forth from child to caregiver and caregiver to child, sometimes creating feedback loops that perpetuate or worsen an emerging problem.

Comment

This case illustrates how and why the use of attachment theories can be useful to conceptualization.

Some clinicians working along the attachment theories have emphasized the utmost importance of the first few months of life when a form of traumatic separation occurs. Some have even attributed to his stay for about a week as a nine-month old infant in difficult conditions, Ted Kaczinski's erratic relationship to the social world that eventually led to his full estrangement and methodical killings.

Kaczinski's mother reported that he was a happy baby when she took him to the hospital but when she brought him home he was limp and unresponsive, "like a bundle of clothes". During his stay, he had to be pinned down by personnel in order to take pictures of his hives and the mother was not allowed to visit.

This is not to say that a baby who goes to the hospital for a week will turn into a murderer or that young children should never leave the side of their caretaker, but that possible disruptions of attachments must be considered if signs, symptoms or behaviors appear, following an event that might have caused a disruption.

For the past fifty years or so, research in developmental psychology has consistently demonstrated that young children and infants have much more sophisticated cognitive abilities and practices than their status of "babies" tends to inspire in us. They are also extremely more vulnerable to external conditions and Melanie Klein has provided a number of observations and hypotheses that begin to give a measure of the intensity with which they experience the world, particularity when this world is perceived as turning against them but also as part of their normal, optimal development.

When there is in the child's history anything that might have constituted such a disruption, it is logically indicated to use attachment theories to investigate the matter, starting with exhaustive history of the circumstances, failing which, there can be no understanding of the child's predicament and no efficient, durable treatment. As a rule, it is always a good idea to scan for such disruptions at intake and to develop a general sense of the corresponding developmental lines.

It is also worth mentioning, again, that parents' alcohol or drug abuse can easily constitute such a disruption as the child, and much more so the infant, will invariably feel an absence even if the parent is physically within proximity. Estranged from the social world through the abuse of substance, the parent will be accurately perceived as such by the attuned child.

As in B's case, children with relational difficulties are also more likely to be sexually abused due to their fragmented boundaries and to their ambivalent need for the other.

Lone Wolf

P was born the first an only child of an unmarried couple. Reports stated that P's parents did not have any significant relationship before or after his birth. Pregnancy was unremarkable but birth was premature by three weeks and infancy positive for "feeding problems," which required P to stay for about two weeks in the hospital.

Developmental milestones were met within average range except for normal control of excretory functions, which was eventually accomplished by age four.

From P's birth to the present, mother and son have lived either on their own, without any paternal figure, or with the maternal grandparents for bouts of about two years in duration (i.e. about six moves total.)

P reportedly became aware of his father at about age eight and has met him only twice. This individual appears to have been rather disturbed and spent several years in prison for burglary and sexual offense. After his release, this man exhibited suicidal behaviors, for which he had to be hospitalized and eventually completed suicide by hanging four years later, this year.

P's mother has a history of suicide, with two attempts, one in her teenage years and the second and last in 2004, when P was about nine, following a miscarriage. She was also reported to have used substances, marijuana but mostly methamphetamine and particularly in 2002-2003, when P was seven or eight years of age. It is also at about that time that sexual issues became apparent. At least two instances of sexual acting out were documented in 2002 between P, then seven, and a twelve-year old boy.

Starting at about the same time, P's behaviors degraded and began to include assaultive behaviors towards his mother and homicidal and suicidal ideation or fantasies, which eventually led to a brief admission to a psychiatric hospital in 2003.

Various interventions were attempted in a variety of settings and placements but were unable to significantly alter P's course toward violent and sexual acting out, in part due to his mother's difficulties accepting and following through the recommendations repeatedly offered by the many professionals involved.

As P's assaultive behaviors towards his mother continued to increase, a long-term residential placement eventually appeared as the only option left.

Of note is P's minimal difficulties in the school environment, where his relationships were still fraught with conflict but where he also appeared to excel, particularly in mathematics. P's latest GPA was 3.63 and his results on the Woodcock-Johnson, Third Edition, placed him at a College level in mathematics.

Data garnered through this evaluation were scarce but appeared to converge in suggesting the presence of an emerging personality disorder of the psychopathic spectrum. Nothing in this evaluation was suggestive of a depressive dynamic, with or without manic defense, or of an anxiety disorder.

Personality disorders are more problematic than other mental disorders as the pathogenic elements, conflicts or fantasies, have pervaded the entire psychology. As a result, personality disordered individuals typically are not aware of the presence of a problem in themselves and are always brought to the attention of clinicians through complaints of others rather than through painful subjective experiences.

The psychopathic spectrum defines individuals who are fascinated by the expression of power for its own sake, are much more preoccupied with self-definition than with relationships and take pleasure in duping others or in subjecting them to manipulation. There are two recognized kinds of psychopathic deviation, the active-aggressive (i.e. predator) and the passive-parasitic (i.e. con-artist), and P seems to vacillate between these two poles, probably due to the relative malleability of his character structure at his still young age.

A sexual component is often present but essentially under the angle of someone's power over someone else. This aspect is concerning as it might lead directly to acts of predation.

The etiology of psychopathic personality disorder is thought to reflect a grave disorder of early or very early attachment. Neglect, abuse, addiction and/or chaotic unreliability in caregivers, and/or a profoundly bad fit between the child's temperament and that of the responsible adult may have made a normal attachment impossible.

In P's case, historical data suggested that a mixture of emotional detachment or absence (e.g. substance abuse) and of compensatory over-indulgence might have constituted such pathogenic environment. As suggested by a protracted anal phase and other test data, it is also probable that P's phallic phase, during which boys see their erection as an expression of their power (i.e. three to four years of age), constitutes a point of fixation.

It is also thought that P sees his intelligence, probably above average, as a symbolic expression of such phallic power, a sword of sorts, that places him in a position of initial superiority over others. However, when placed in a position where his power is challenged, mostly by females, P is likely to react very violently in order to reassert his sense of superiority.

Prognosis is typically guarded to poor, at least in the short term, for this type of disorder and long-term treatment will likely be necessary to effect significant and sustained behavioral change.

Psychotherapy should avoid the insight-oriented angle, as this is likely to be interpreted by P as a sign of weakness from the therapist, while the acquired knowledge would be used to strengthen his fantasized power rather than to expose it to critical testing and insight.

The cognitive, social-learning based, models are also likely to be inefficient, as P will master the skills very quickly, which he probably already has, but covertly and systematically use loopholes and gray areas, thus preventing internalization, strengthening his sense of superiority and in effect deceiving the treatment purpose.

Comment

Out of the hundreds of children I have encountered, perhaps four or five clearly belonged to the antisocial or psychopathic spectrum, which I tend to define as a general estrangement from the emotional aspect of the social world. These children have reduced sensitivity to the other on an emotional level but are often very perceptive of all other aspects of social relationships, which differentiates them clearly from autistic individuals or from other forms of estrangements brought about by other psychological issues.

These children, and the adults they become, are therefore basically alone, isolated from the network of connections that human life creates around itself. I conceptualize them as a product of severe attachment issues and of epigenetics. Somehow, primal survival genes or functions seem to have been expressed, turned on by their circumstances, which results in a "lone wolf" vision of the World. The development of their narcissism has been arrested and is fixated anywhere between the level of an infant and that of a two or three year old. As usual, the most archaic the fixation, the more severe the estrangement.

With these individuals, the clinician reaches an unknown territory, where all available practices become inefficient or even counter-productive. As with all others pathologies that evolve from early to very early disturbances of human development, too little is known to even begin to build operational theories and society has no positive outlet to offer.

The fact that there are so many neglected and abused children but so few psychopathic ones speaks for little humans' ability to suck out of their environment the little substance they need to maintain a minimal level of connection to their species.

Staff's Little Boy

Seven-year old boy short stature, thin and strong. Admitted from foster-care where his behaviors were deemed unmanageable. Outburst of anger and aggression, lack of social interaction including with peers across settings, voluntary under-use of verbal communication, archaic behaviors such as hoarding food, eating and licking inappropriate objects, such as eating dog-food and licking windows, dissociative behaviors, such as blank stare or sudden collapse in fetal position, negative reaction to affectionate touch and praise, appears to enjoy aggression, compulsively orderly.

W's life was very poorly documented until he entered the system but it appears that for the first six to nine months, he was living with both his parents who then separated. The child began to be bounced around between his mother, father, other family and friends. Social services intervened at the request of W's grandmother, who felt unable to care appropriately for him. Followed many foster-care placements with occasional stays with the grandmother but W's behaviors steadily deteriorated and he was eventually admitted for residential treatment.

Prior to his admission, he was, rightly, diagnosed with a reactive attachment disorder, a much better assessment than the bipolar disorder he was treated for, but as customary, the evaluation culminated in a diagnosis and didn't contain any recommendation or dynamic interpretation.

The few data available at this time converged in describing a clinical picture dominated by the presence of features typical of a reactive attachment disorder of the inhibited type. However, data also suggested that there might have been enough healthy attachment and enough quality parenting in infancy to create a stable core to W's psychological structure.

This positive aspect seemed related to his mother, the loss of whom fostered the development of a depressive dynamic, which would then also suggest that the attachment disorder features might have an etiology chronologically posterior to infancy thus improving prognosis and accounting for the hints of resilience observed with W.

In particular, some data suggested that W has a relatively structured super-ego, thus decreasing the odds of the radical estrangement usually evolving from similar life-circumstances into an oppositional or a conduct disorder.

W's intense anger would therefore be dominantly regressive and therefore an expression of despair and depression, a cry for help rather than an automatic, self-preserving and preemptive mechanism. Regression does appear as W's main coping strategy, which the presence of enuresis and other symptoms supports.

Other data (e.g. report of being a "neat-freak") also suggested the possibility of obsessive-compulsive traits and therefore of neurotic anxiety, another positive indicator of psychological structure, as opposed to primitive paranoid-schizoid anxiety. W's insistence at blackening parts of his drawing inside the borders then could be seen as his compulsive attempt at controlling the possibility of an explosive and catastrophic release of anger.

W's anxiety could also explain his general cautious demeanor (e.g. slow and light movements, soft voice) including his ritualistic walking on the tip of his toes.

There were also a few indicators of regression to an earlier, oral, level such as thumb-sucking with dissociation, hoarding or selective mutism. W's out-of-control behaviors can be seen as containing a measure of archaic oral aggression.

In sum, it is thought that after a few relatively stable months, probably six to twelve, which were enough to allow W to evolve from an archaic position with fragmented internal objects to a more advanced position with more stable, whole internal objects, his environment began to fall apart. W's psychosexual development thereby was stunted and marked by incomplete achievements of the oral and anal phase, which seems to represent the highest level he has reached and therefore the level of his current fixation.

At the same time, probably due to extreme inconsistencies, emotional unavailability of his parents, basic neglect and probable violence, W's object-relational development was similarly stunted, with internal objects remaining in their primitive, simplest and unstable form, and resulted in the interruption of the development of his ability to bond and to communicate.

This state of affairs places W's caretakers in the position of parents even more so than is common with disturbed children and the largest part of his treatment will need to be a form of re-parenting, bringing him through the relevant phases of his psychological development.

This means that staff will have to start at W's current lowest level of development and not assume that standard implementation of a social-learning model will work. Such lowest level is thought to be at around nine to twelve month-old, therefore non-verbal, which is also seen as part of the reason why W seldom uses words to communicate.

At this age, processing of incoming stimuli is still accomplished primarily through the brainstem and the diencephalon, meaning that only simple functions are involved, such as arousal, motor regulation, appetite, and various autonomic functions (e.g. heart rate.) These are the areas of the brain and the functions that will be primarily activated when W will react to an unpleasant situation. Very secondarily, and depending on the intensity of the stimulus, processing will reach the limbic system and include emotions, while little or no processing will take place in the cortex, where logical thinking and inhibition take place.

This means that W will likely be unresponsive to commands, logical arguments or verbal explanation, while he will respond to non-verbal cues. Tone of voice should be very low, rate very slow and words limited to the smallest possible number (e.g. "No", "Yes",) while facial expressions would be considered as the main vector of communication.

It will take a very large number of repetitions and positive experiences to extend the average processing to the level of the limbic system which is W's chronological level of development at eight years of age, allowing the addition of emotional reactivity and attachment and facilitating elementary, concrete, cortical processing.

On a psychosexual level, W will probably vacillate between oral regression, with aggression and chaotic feeding and anal regression with behavioral explosions and stubbornness. Typical parenting methods involving, strict schedules, consistency and patience are recommended. Of course, power-struggles should be avoided and replaced with negotiation. A good indicator of W's progress through these phases would be of course, bladder control but also the appearance of attempts at splitting male from female staff, thus heralding the re-working of the oedipal phase.

In order to consolidate and reinforce W's fragile and unstable internal objects, every female interacting with W will have to become a substitute of his mother and every male a substitute of his father. Within this perspective and with the goal of pulling W upward by establishing a coherent, stable and consistent parental pole, it could be helpful to have a male and female staff interacting together, as a unit, with W as much as possible.

Play-therapy is recommended and the psychotherapist is encouraged to let W develop his own play while observing closely his actions, as it is likely that W will project his inarticulate conflicts and anxieties in such play. Comments and/or interpretations and/or hypotheses on what W could be alluding to or unconsciously expressing could prove useful by fostering verbalization.

Implementation of these recommendations will have to navigate around a risk of infantilization, which W might also be using to cling to his regressed states. W is likely to stimulate in staff working with him an unconscious protective, parental fiber which might therefore be counter-productive. The idea is not to treat W as an infant or a toddler but to establish communication with his brain at its current dominant level of processing.

Until W has reached, and settled in, a chronologically appropriate emotional, cognitive and behavioral level, a high level of care is likely to be required. Rushing into discharge to a lower level of care without clear facts demonstrating the above would likely result in another failed placement and would considerably worsen W's overall prognosis.

Comment

This case illustrates how a spectacular clinical picture can evolve from a relatively well organized psychological structure. It offers a counter-point to case 15 where a benign presentation covered up a deep disturbance.

As predicted, staff's counter-transference to W was very intense, which translated into a tendency to care for him more than was needed, which W quickly realized and used. The same counter-transference was of course present in W's adoptive candidates and turned into feelings of resentment and anger when W began to test their true motivation and to violently attack their fantasized love for the abused child.

W, a defective product, was "returned" to the facility, his true family, where his ambivalence was tolerated and his regression a sure way of keeping it together. He was still there six years after the evaluation.

Like W, some children, through what is known of their history or through some of their features or unconscious communication, have the power to elicit extremely powerful counter-transferences in others, all of them revolving around semiconscious to unconscious narratives of rescue. These are the same children who create conflicts, sometime very intense as well, among the individual in charge of their case or treatment. I have seen professionals nearly coming to blows over such cases.

One can argue that for W, living in a facility was the best option and that might well be the case, but from a clinical perspective, he was, as I feared, infantilized and validated in his regressive state, which will translate later into behavioral and relational problems.

Also, as illustrated by several of the cases presented in this collection, a disorder of the attachment is not necessarily a Reactive Attachment Disorder which is a diagnostic category primarily inspired by the extreme end of the spectrum. In such cases, attachment is simply the developmental line that offers the most intelligent and efficient way of conceptualizing the clinical picture and, hopefully, to inspire the child's treatment.

The Reluctance to Talk about "It"

Tall, stocky, resistant fifteen year old admitted against his mother's will. Mother very reluctant to share any personal, historical information and S, expectedly, not very cooperative either. Chronology was obtained by cross-referencing mother's account, son's account and previous data were minimal due to pervasive resistance.

As can be seen, data were extremely scarce but however converged in suggesting plausible etiological hypotheses. One such hypothesis would be an early sexual abuse, which would most probably have remained unprocessed, in part due to P's early age at the time (i.e. four-years old) and would have fostered a very strong ambivalence about sexuality and a vacillation between active and passive, male and female role, as observed in P today.

Another such hypothesis would see P's physical abuse at the hands of his father as the primary cause, the vacillating identification between the victimized mother and the abusive father evolving into, again, female and male, passive and active roles.

This effect would have been reinforced if the physical abuse had taken place within the Oedipal stage, between age three and five or six, since it would directly impact the child's psychosexual evolution by associating gender roles with domination and submission through physical or sexual violence. It is even possible that a sado-masochistic component associating pleasure and pain with role-reversal would have evolved from such circumstances.

The depressive component, observed and implicit in P's history of suicidal ideation would also find its origin in the loss of the father as caring, uplifting and structuring figure and in the internalizing of a sexually and/or physically aggressive male.

This component, however, along with the post-traumatic element, is thought to have been integrated over time, resulting in an emerging narcissistic/histrionic structure with projection and denial as main defenses. As a result, these etiological aspects are now inaccessible, as they have, as it were, dissolved into P's personality, leaving him in conscious control of a large part of his negative behaviors but oblivious to their ancient origin.

Finally, the arousal obtained through either submission (i.e. with males) or domination (i.e. with females) appears to have created a self-perpetuating reward system continually fueling P's personality development in the same pathological direction.

Gender identity and sexual life are thought to sit at the core of P's psychological and behavioral problems. Therefore, it is thought that change will only take place to the extent that these areas are verbally processed. This task is likely to be difficult, however, due to P's narcissistic denial and projection, his organized defensiveness and his intelligence.

An entry point would be to focus on the fantasized association between female position and submission and male position and domination and to explore their connection with sexual excitement and fantasies, as well as their expressions in P's everyday life, including interactions with peers and staff at school or on unit.

Individual psychotherapy is likely to reflect the dynamic between domination and submission, and P's psychotherapist will probably experience such oscillations in his/her counter-transference and subjective experience in session.. This aspect is reinforced by P's current situation in a treatment facility where he is required to "submit" to authority (i.e. accept).

However, reality-therapy appears to constitute a more appropriate option for P's treatment, as character psychotherapy is extremely long and difficult, while relatively little time is left to bring P's negative behaviors under a measure of control (see W. Glasser, 1967).

On unit, it is also recommended that particular attention be paid to interactions with P, which should be as neutral as possible in order to strip the exercise of staff's authority of as much stimulation as possible. Either friendliness or hostility would increase P's arousal and validate his dynamic a little more. This is recommended because staff naturally tend to humanize interactions, which is very helpful in most cases but not with P for the reasons described above.

Comment

In many cases, ranging from simple neurotic to severe personality issues, sexuality sits at the core of the conceptualization and of the treatment. Unfortunately, since the demise of psychoanalysis very few psychotherapist are able to broach these issues with their Patients in the matter-of-fact, open and neutral manner required for their processing. Comparable to "a physician examining an armpit" as Freud used to say. Sexual issues are by and large ignored, or displaced and only tolerated by clinicians when related to sexual abuse. Even in these cases, processing remains very limited and tends to be expedited as fast and as superficially as possible, which contributes to leaving already reluctant victims in a state of validated repression.

I remember the case of an eleven year old girl brought to treatment by her father following the sudden irruption of obsessive-compulsive behaviors, such as checking her room several times before going to bed, insisting to sleep with her parents, between them, anxiety attacks and so forth. Her father, a physician, was concerned that her symptoms would be the first signs of a serous disorder.

It was rather obvious that this young girl was rehashing Oedipal issues exacerbated by her emerging sexuality. The clinician working with her reported to me that she had spent half of her first session running her index finger around and inside an artificial orchid that was sitting on the clinician's desk, a behavior very transparent, a confession of sorts and a mute cry for help in relation to masturbation.

The clinician felt embarrassed and did not interpret or help her verbalize and elaborate but released her to her father with the standard reassurance that there was no disorder he could find, that her behaviors would abate and were probably caused by the first wave of the hormonal changes of adolescence.

In this case the consequence of not broaching the sexual issue is almost negligible but in the case of a victim of sexual abuse, it amounts to a dismissal or to a tacit agreement with the abuser that such a secret should indeed be left unspoken.

This case also illustrates the fascination young boys develop for a violent father, most particularly when such violence is somehow associated to sexuality. Depending on a number of factors such as the intensity of such violence and/or of the sexual component, the developmental level of the child at the time of exposure, etc. this can lead to very severe difficulties later in life.

These difficulties invariably revolve around fantasies of homosexual submission and heterosexual domination and are often difficult to conceptualize from the signs and symptoms initially presented. One of my patients eventually hung himself soon after his nineteen birthday following five or six years of attempts at compensation through self-injury or mutilation (i.e. piercing his own penis) and grandiose fantasies of domination and superiority, which his above average intelligence facilitated.

Therapy with him was exceedingly difficult because any advance, gain or any positive transference, simultaneously endorsed the meaning of a defeat, of a humiliating submission to my male power. He knew I was benevolent but the fantasy was buried too deeply and had been organized for too long. Adolescence had solidified and locked dynamics that might have been accessible earlier.

On our last monthly session, I had the feeling he had made up his mind about something and repeated to him that we could move past his difficulties and that I was available to him. He thanked me with a smirk. I suspect he had progressively practiced auto-erotic asphyxiation, possibly as a way of getting closer to the final act, of which the little boy in him was naturally terrified. Eventually, he went out with an erection as powerful and final as death itself.

I'm a Big Girl

Fourteen-year old girl admitted due to ongoing uncontrollable behaviors, most particularly no less than 15 elopements over the past year. Her parents separated before her birth and a step-father came into the picture two-years later. Behavioral problems appeared in the school as early as first grade and two years later, at age nine, Y disclosed that the stepfather had been sexually using her and her older sister.

The couple of course divorced and the man was sent to prison. After a brief period of calm, Y's behaviors sharply escalated at around age 10, a time at which she also matured physically. The situation steadily degraded over the next three years in spite of an attempt at placement with her biological father in another State and of several temporary stays in group homes and shelters for youth. Of course. substance use and abuse developed simultaneously, including with her father, who allowed her to consume alcohol and cannabis.

Y's symptoms, signs and behaviors seem to have their root in the conflictual and ambivalent relationship she had with her abusive stepfather. It is believed that the sexual aspect of this relationship has been insufficiently processed, if at all, and that the non-sexual aspect might have been entirely overlooked.

The suspected depressive component, carefully repressed by Y but plainly visible when observing her and interacting with her, is thought to originate in the symbolic loss of the caring, uplifting and structuring father-figure for the confusing and over-stimulating one, probably at an earlier age than the reported abuse. Y's earliest memory of her stepfather was dated age five and it is suspected that this is also at about that age that the abusive father-figure began to overtake the other.

It is also at around that age that oedipal issues are at their highest, with children becoming aware of their parents' relationship, of sexual differences and entertaining fantasies of supplanting the rival parent. As a result, girls often become more flirtatious and physical with their father, which a pedophile would use for his own immediate gratification rather than as a necessary frustration and structuring phase for the child.

The resulting "Oedipal Triumph" has many toxic consequences, such as realizing the child's fantasies, which leads to the development of an undue sense of one's power and often in a severe sense of entitlement. It also prevents the child to identify with the mother, whom she replaces with the father, thus thwarting emotional and identity development. The symbolic loss of the pre-genital mother then also contributes to reinforce the depressive dynamic. It might also take unconscious fantasies a step further, by including, for example, fantasized "babies," often translated into eating symptoms or conversion symptoms (e.g. Y's abdominal problems.) The irruption of puberty, when sexual characteristics become obvious, also often triggers a sharp escalation in symptoms, signs and behaviors.

The "real/unreal" situation lived by the child often promotes the use of pervasive, rather than reactive (i.e. coping with acute trauma,) dissociation, as illustrated by Y's results on the TSCC, while a general sense of confusion about reality is frequently observed.

As in Y's case, this situation is complicated when, aside from the fulfillment of fantasy, the incest is kept secret for a long time and/or contains pleasant aspects (e.g. involuntary physiological reactions,) as guilt, often fostered by the perpetrator, then develops and prevents full access to the trauma, locking the victim in a state of permanent denial and/or hysterical repression.

Y clearly showed, in the way she endorsed items on the MACI and in her behaviors since she reached puberty, that denial, repression and acting out were indeed the way she deals with the continuing and intensified confusion she experiences about who she really is, who others really are, what is really being done and by whom. Y's vacillations between childish seductiveness and overly mature demeanor and ideation while interacting with psychologist illustrated such unconscious confusion.

Y's insistence on her genetic similarity to a father who was absent most of her life and her stated desire to go live with him can be understood in this perspective as her desperate attempt at summoning a father-image that would cover-up or overpower her ambivalent and guilty attachment to her abusive stepfather.

Individual psychotherapy can be helpful to the extent that it allows anamnesis (i.e. remembering) and verbalization of the incest in all its aspects, including and particularly the ones that also had a positive value, and therefore a guilt-inducing quality, for Y (e.g. loving relationship, secret kept, pleasurable sensations.)

Y's resistance will probably be very strong, as she has been practicing denial, repression and acting-out defenses for several years. Such unconscious defenses are likely to be perceived by Y as personality features (i.e. "who I am",) and she will probably reject any direct attempt at interpreting them as an attempt at "changing" her. Only patient and tactful confrontations on inconsistencies (e.g. elopements resulting in loss of freedom) will erode Y's resistance.

A possible entry point would be the patient investigation of the period before the abuse was disclosed, memories about the relationship when it was not sexually abusive, with the goal of stimulating Y's positive feelings about her stepfather. If this is accomplished, guilt should be directly elicited, thus opening the way to deeper interpretations.

Transference to the female psychotherapist is likely to be negative at first and contempt is likely to be present although probably hidden under a façade of indifference, as if saying "You are not powerful enough to compete with me". In a second phase, contempt might shift more explicitly towards anger and frustration. A marker of successful psychotherapy would be the emergence of a positive transference, with material suggesting imitation and competition with the psychotherapist.

Once minimal individual work accomplished, family counseling will be advisable to extend the processing to the whole family structure, possibly including Y's biological father. It is likely, in particular, that Y's mother experiences, symmetrically to her daughter, very large amounts of guilt. Y's father should also become more aware of the very large symbolic meaning and power he holds for his daughter and therefore of his responsibilities.

Comment

In cases like this one, where the incestuous situation was kept secret for a long time, the child has had to organize a very compartmentalized world, which is only possible by very consistent decision-making, which itself gives the child an undue, age inappropriate, but very real sense of agency and control over her life. Consequently, these children typically are either very introverted or, when extroverted, typically reject requests from authority, leading to impulsive acting out such as elopements.

When she was running away from her home, Y was not an oppositional thirteen-year old but a six-year old pretending she was an autonomous adult making decisions for herself.

This is the only logical way to understand why an otherwise intelligent teenager would consistently, fifteen times in about a year, put herself in situations where it was obvious she would get caught and suffer further restriction to her freedom.

Again, this state of affairs was made possible by the lack of thorough processing of the many facets of her incestuous relationship with her stepfather at a time where she was still malleable enough to alter her course.

Humiliated Rage

Sixteen year old boy admitted for long-term residential treatment and for the second time since age ten. His first residential placement was nearly two-years long. He presented as a thin boy or average height who had not reached puberty, which considering his age was out of range.

He was generally uncooperative during the assessment, probably because he had just been admitted. For most of the others, an initial evaluation made the rapport easier, as they had not yet developed a view of the map and were both uncertain and curious, as children typically are, but in his case that was the opposite. As a result I had few and not very reliable data.

His father was in prison, as he had been on and off for all of R's life. His mother was raising two siblings by herself and R had been returned to treatment after he had assaulted her with a metal bar, an aggravated assault. He had a rather long history of problems including burglary, property destruction, assault on others, including a five-year old, academic failure, all of which having resumed immediately after his discharge from the previous residential facility.

His mother had reported that she had a very close bond with R and that he was often behaving like an "abusive husband". There was no male figure in R's life aside form his imprisoned father.

Test data converged in describing an adolescent with severe, long-term dysthymia and a co-morbid anxiety disorder. Throughout his endorsement of the items of three different instruments, R consistently described himself as a dejected, pessimistic and withdrawn adolescent with anorexic and hypochondriacal tendencies. The general image resulting from his self-report was that of a hapless, worried and at times despairing victim of his circumstances.

However, these results are in stark contrast with R's history over the past four to five years which described a consistently defiant, at times seriously assaultive teenager with an already long series of documented criminal behaviors across settings.

It is also important to remember that R has a long history of psychotherapeutic and psycho-social interventions, including nearly two years of placement in the institution which branded the treatment model currently used by St. Joe's and including several evaluations, psychological or psychiatric, with several professionals. In other words, R is treatment-savvy and probably able to project a particular image.

In the sub-field of forensic psychology, criminal behavior is assessed and rated not in the view of the results of psychological test or batteries but as a function of the degree of discrepancy between these results and collateral sources. This method came to predominate due to these individuals' tendency to utilize psychological testing as a means of skirting responsibility, minimizing their actions and projecting a victimized image.

Without suggesting going to such extreme with R, it is thought however that the discrepancy between the innocent, generally suffering and self-debasing image he projected across tests and interviews and the consistency of the significant conduct problems he has displayed over the last several years gives a better estimate of his dynamics than test results alone.

R's dominantly introversive personality profile described in the section above is the only result consistent with this interpretation.

As a result, it appears that R presents with a Conduct Disorder based on several emerging narcissistic and anti-social personality traits. Etiology for such disorders is typically very archaic with probable dysfunction, traumatic or chronic within the first year of life and is therefore often impossible to document with certainty.

The dysthymic layer is thought to be two-fold, with a superficial, reactive and largely engineered layer, due to R's current circumstances and a much deeper, unconscious component, which will remain inaccessible to psychotherapy as long as the conduct disorder organization will prevail.

On the whole, this evaluation suggested that R's case is a difficult one, with a very experienced patient and dynamics buried under thick layers of asocial defenses. Prognosis is therefore very guarded.

Comment

After a couple of months of acceptable behaviors, R began to act out, in particular in the school where he was assaultive to others and where he had to be restrained on several occasions. These restraints were remarkable in that they lasted for a very long time, with this relatively small boy wrestling on the floor with several grown and trained men for half an hour or more. The violence began to carry over to his unit and staff felt that he had to be transferred to the secure unit until he calmed down.

A couple of months after this transfer, R committed suicide in his room.

I was not involved in R's treatment aside from my initial evaluation so I didn't pay enough attention to the evolution of his behaviors, which I attributed to his conduct disorder. I didn't re-read my own evaluation nor was I asked to look at his behaviors. If I had, I would have probably be alerted by the intensity of his acting out which would have brought me to realize that it was fueled by humiliated rage and was a defense against very painful narcissistic injuries. And if I had realized that, I would have warned that suicidal gestures were indeed likely.

Looking back at what I wrote, I see that I didn't put enough weight on the narcissistic component of his emerging personality and on his terrible vulnerability to perceived slight, which his being very much behind in his hormonal development certainly exacerbated.

Perhaps a day or two before he killed himself, I haphazardly ran into him on his unit. He walked towards me and said with a smile: "You don't like me do you?", to which I responded: "No I do. You remind me of a Roman soldier", which he did with his crown of curly hair. He laughed and asked if that was true, which it was. He looked relaxed and happy, a far cry from the boy that was cussing and fighting with staff a couple of days earlier. He had made up his mind.

I think that humiliated rage is the fuel of any severe explosion of anger, be it against oneself, against others or both. This is the factor to look for when there is a doubt of serious acting out. Even in the case of methodical serial killers, I think it is somewhere in their history, accumulates, brews and simmers and gets released when acting out provides a strong enough compensation.

Many psychological issues do or can translate into violence and all involve at least some disconnection from reality but, even in the case of active psychosis or paranoid delusions, severe violence, homicidal or suicidal violence, will in my view always come from humiliated rage.

This seems to suggest that developmental lines and theories looking at narcissism, ala Kohut or Kernberg, should be used primarily when assessing actual risk.

Another lesson taught by R is that any abrupt change or dramatic improvement seen in an otherwise depressed or disturbed individual is highly likely to be a warning sign of impending acting-out. I become very worried when I see a depressed or anxious patient who suddenly does "great". The feeling of surprised I experience at the report is my warning sign.

Last Stop before Adulthood

Fourteen-year old boy who was admitted following a year of falling asleep in class and cannabis use. The magnitude of this boy's hypersomnia in class, but never at home, and its intractability eventually determined his being placed in the State's custody.

C's mother raised her three children, of whom C is the last, "mostly" by herself. She also reported having been an alcoholic until C was about five. There was little or no help from the father. C was reported to have been "Mom's baby" for about ten years.

Behavioral problems started at around that time, which also coincided with C's transition to Middle School and its period system. At about the same time, C's mother went through a depressive episode, brought about by "thyroid instability" and "serious" surgery on her breasts. At that time and for a few months, she reported becoming "withdrawn" and "in bed a lot."

At around that time, C's six-year old cousin was molested by a neighbor boy whom C knew, which according to his mother seemed to impact him as he seemed to "hold on to things" much more after that.

Still at that time, C's current stepfather joined the family but was reported to also have alcohol abuse issues.

Finally, a few months ago, as C transitioned from Middle School to High School, his mother suffered violent attacks of migraines and had to stop working. It is at that time that C's behaviors began to evolve into what they were at admission.

Data garnered from multiple sources converged in suggesting a dominant depressive dynamic with co-morbid anxiety disorder and suspected molestation issues. The etiology of the depressive/anxious formation is thought to originate in the combination of young C's symbolic loss of his mother when she was emotionally absent due to her bouts of inebriation and of his anxious attachment to the loving and anxious mother at other times.

Within this context, C's closed-in attitude can be seen as a calm and collected front created to support and reassure his anxious and probably guilty mother. Such systematic "holding-back" has been repeatedly described by various observers and pervaded the data of this evaluation, which suggests that it has become a character trait, deeply ingrained in C's personality.

C's most recent symptom, his sleeping in class is thought to be a primarily a sign of severe insomnia and an unconscious, symbolic and aggressive statement directed at his mother, as if saying, "So now you know how it feels (felt) when you're passed out, can't wake up, can't be with me." It is a compromise between a loving component (i.e. worrying about mother's well-being), an aggressive component (i.e. retaliating on mother) and a guilt component (i.e. failing at school, self-defeating.)

The obsessive worrying which facilitates the insomnia appears self-medicated with alcohol or cannabis, thus, again, emulating mother's past behaviors (i.e. being mother's "baby") while retaliating on her.

Data, particularly from the Rorschach suggested the presence of an explosive potential, which has to some extent been documented through offensive, aggressive and at times assaultive behaviors. However, there were also indications that C's explosions are felt with relief by him and have historically been relatively mild in intensity. This group of data, along with the "holding-back" and the obsessive worrying points towards a powerful anal-retentive dynamic fostered by the early need to contain anxiety.

Data from the Rorschach also suggested a relatively intact and stable psychological structure and the ability to perceive the world in a conventional and accurate manner.

C's refusal to elaborate about the sexual molestation of his young cousin by a neighborhood boy and his angry rejection of any discussion, even superficial, about sexual matters makes it difficult to reject the possibility of a molestation, perhaps by the same perpetrator. However, the dynamics offered above seem to suggest a more operational alternative explanation for C's "holding to things" and have the advantage of being firmly established in his biography.

The failure of past psychotherapeutic efforts with C might have rested on the superficial intention to extract information from him, which represented a frontal attack on his anal-retentive dominant defense. It appears that tackling the defense itself and first could be a more productive approach with C, particularly if his intelligence and strong curiosity can be enlisted in the process.

More generally, it is likely that psychotherapy with C will resemble a "potty training war" with the psychotherapist in the position of the training mother requesting that C indulge her by giving her his material. In such perspective, C's stubborn refusal is seen as a regressive retaliation on her for not being there. This is likely to be more active with females (i.e. more immediate mother-figures) than with males.

Strong ambivalence to his mother appears as the most likely central issue to process and verbalize in psychotherapy, which of course extends to family psychotherapy as well. Revisiting C's earlier years with his mother, through mother's participation and recollection, would be helpful to this process. This is all the more true given C's mother feelings of guilt, which should be dealt with first to avoid repeating the cycle of indulgence/retaliation. It is also probable that such guilt played an important role in C's negative behaviors by fostering looser disciplining and perhaps by splitting C's parents and limiting C's father interventions, which, if confirmed, should also be systematically explored.

This last point needs to be stressed since the lack of a father-figure in C's early life did play a very significant role in his intricate relationship with his mother, who was a single-parent, while issues of identity development will absolutely require the active involvement of a father-figure for the next few years if further behavioral and psychological problems are to be avoided. Therefore, the authority of C's father needs to be validated, re-instated and acknowledged without any restriction, which his bouts of alcohol abuse had made difficult or impossible until recently.

If/when C's anal defenses soften, a depressive undercurrent will probably begin to surface, only then lending itself to verbalization and processing.

C's psychotherapist should also remain alert to the possibility that a form of trauma related to molestation might play a role in C's current psychological problems. At the minimum, and when C and his psychotherapist will have reached a level of mutual comfort, C's over-reaction to sexual matters could be tactfully investigated.

Similar issues of stubbornness, passive-resistance will probably be seen on unit but this evaluation did not suggest any reason why a significant alteration to the facility's milieu and standard model would be needed to deal with them.

Similar issues will also probably be observed in the school, which is the place of choice where children are required to "produce" on demand. In this environment, which is the environment where C chose to display his dominant symptom (e.g. sleeping everyday, failing), his above average intellectual abilities should be consistently and systematically pushed to their limit. A minimum level of achievement consistent with such abilities (e.g. 90%) should be part of his treatment plan and discharge criteria.

Comment

This case also illustrates the turning point represented by the sixteenth year. This the time where adolescents are beginning their active transition towards adulthood, autonomy and self-referenced responsibility. They can drive, they can legally earn money, they can legally drop out and if they don't, they are expected to take over their academic work and symbolically, their destiny. For many teenagers, this is felt not as the onset of the freedom they claim they want but as the end of childhood, which sometimes severely impacts some of them, particularly when there are dormant issues.

For some teenagers, this situation extends until the very last year of high school in a sort of wishful moratorium and I have seen several cases where the adolescent drops out just a few months or even a few weeks short of graduation.

It is the rule that the dominant issue will produce at that time the dominant symptom, which itself enfolds the dominant conflict carried over from ancient times.

C's is yet another mild case that might have been successfully dealt with in the community if available resources had allowed conceptualization and tailored interventions. Interventions were tried but they didn't rely on a conceptualization of the case and were therefore as many shots in the dark.

Ironically as well, placement at the highest level of care didn't allow much more and C's psychiatric institutionalization merely offered a clean break from his world and history, which is certainly positive in itself, and therapeutic in many cases, but without much of a clinical determination or intent. Similar results, or even better results, would have been achieved through an extended stay in summer camp in a remote location.

Adrift

Fourteen-year old girl Lakota on her mother's side and white on her, unknown, father side. A's mother's sister and her husband took A in when she was about a year old, as mother was an alcoholic and led an erratic life on the Reservation.

When A was eight, her beloved uncle died. A's problems became apparent when she turned twelve and reached menarche. At that time, "I don't know why, my mood changed." She started to drink, to gravitate towards kids "like me" (i.e. not white, not rich, poor students), to use drugs and to party. She also began to drift toward the family of her dead uncle, living quite far from where she was and where she later eloped.

During her most recent elopement, A went to a party where she got drunk, smoked marijuana and was taken advantage of, raped, by an acquaintance.

Dysthymic dynamic possibly rooted in infancy with an unstable, alcoholic mother and successfully contained through childhood, in part due to the important role played by A's uncle. This man was also A's initiator to the Old Ways and his death, when she was about eight years old certainly represented a second loss, which revived and actualized her endemic depressive dynamic. Her identity as a Lakota was possibly partially formed through this relationship, was lost when it ended, and does not seem to have been strengthened since, thus leaving a gaping void and marking still another loss.

A's menarche heralded the end of her identity as a child and the associated loss compounded previous losses and fostered the development of a full-blown symptomatic dysthymia with irritability, self-destructive behaviors and a general indifferent, passive, anhedonic, attitude.

One can see in A's drift toward the "misfit" non-white groups and toward her uncle's family a symbolic attempt at reconnecting with him and with her Lakota identity.

Finally, the possibility of a traumatic (i.e. sexual) etiology to A's symptoms and behaviors needs to be kept in mind due to the presence of a few red-flags (e.g. severe sleeping difficulty, enuresis, tension) and of a recent report of sexual abuse.

Test results suggested that A organized her personality around principles of passive, somewhat manipulative submission and denial, thus building a protective wall around herself but simultaneously isolating herself from rewarding relationships.

A's substance use has the clear characteristics of an anti-depressant self-medication but also contains elements of emulation of her mother's image and thus speaks to this probably very ambivalent fantasized bond which should be explored as well and will probably be strongly projected in the transference.

As suggested above, it is suspected that a central issue to A's behavioral deterioration over the last couple of years was in large part an actualized depressive reaction to the loss of her uncle and it is probable that grieving of this important father figure, now that A is old enough to accomplish such task, would be helpful. Considering that cultural identity issues are intertwined in this clinical issue, it is of note that such grieving process might be better served if carried out the Lakota way in addition to psychotherapy.

Treatment-wise, her therapist's attention is also drawn to the likelihood that A's projected initial receptiveness to therapy and compliance with the "(white) doctor," may create the misleading impression that progress will be rapid. She will seek a dependent relationship with her therapist and, despite promises to the contrary, she will resist efforts to guide her into assuming independence and autonomy. If her therapist is not aware of this aspect of her current personality, A will likely withdraw her emotional investment in therapy, become cold and cynical and produce exclusively what she thinks the therapist wants to hear.

Comment

Identity issues just cannot be ignored with children and adolescents belonging to a minority. In A's case, as in all the other cases of minority kids I came across, they were and she returned to her environment basically unchanged. She did not belong to a psychiatric facility anyway.

To the frustration of working for theory-blind people, minority kids' cases add the frustration of working with "'color-blind" people, meaning people who conveniently deny that there is such a thing as racism and therefore validate its surreptitious, invisible presence. This is a sure way of estranging a child who knows for a fact what she lives.

Home Alone

Ten-year old girl admitted from foster-care placement following violent outbursts, physical aggression towards her younger brother alternating with over-protective behaviors, self-injury and generally unmanageable behaviors. An explosion during which B caused substantial damage to her foster-home to the point that Law Enforcement had to be called, resulted in an admission to the closest psychiatric hospital and from there to long-term residential treatment.

This outbursts happened reportedly "out of nowhere" but the foster-family, along with Family Services also seemed to consider B as a hindrance to the positive development observed in her younger brother and basically wanted her out of the home.

B was born the middle child of a couple who separated and reconciled numerous times, lived in poverty and seemed to have moved from State to State in order to find better circumstances and also probably in order to evade the consequences of the numerous reports of neglect filed against them over many years.

As a result, very little or nothing was known about B's early life and the few data available came from B herself and the memory she had of erratic conditions, "dumpster diving"expeditions to feed the family, violence and drugs in the home.

A year after their placement, B and her younger brother were on their way to being adopted when B's behaviors escalated. B's mother had relinquished her parental rights for the two younger children and had stated in Court that she would choose B's older brother over them.

The central feature, towards which most data appeared to converge, is B's very high level of ambivalence in her perception of, and relationship to, her mother, which appears to be associated with primitive, pre-verbal psychological formations, such as one could find in a very young child, perhaps even an infant.

The oral aspect of this dynamic is prevalent as demonstrated by several lines of data (e.g. Rorschach's last percept, large mouth on drawings, B's seeking solace in food) and constitutes the deepest underlying stratum of B's psychological organization. It appears that more elaborate levels of psycho-sexual developments such as oedipal and anal only constitute transient way-points towards the oral center of B dynamics.

Test data, history and observations suggested that B's regressive drive towards the oral stage is centered around a positive relationship, real or fantasized, with her mother, which unfolded at some point in B's life, probably before age two and exists in B's unconscious as a sort of "lost paradise."

Having lost this paradise due to her mother's erratic life, her multiple abusive and/or neglectful boyfriends, to life in poverty and to the birth of a younger brother, B experienced bitterness, anger, despair and a sense of betrayal in proportion to the amount of love and hope she had invested as a very little girl. Probably out of intense guilt for the terrible angry feelings such ambivalence generate, in an attempt to rehabilitate her mother to her own eyes and to preserve a displaced glimpse of her lost paradise, B seems to have identified with her mother, for example becoming possessive (i.e. protective/abusive) of her younger brother. B's brutal and violent outburst erupted when such compensatory structure collapsed at the sight of her younger sibling improving, surrounded by the normal care and affection of their foster-family, leaving her, again, abandoned, motherless and betrayed.

B's need to impersonate a mother-figure as a means of preserving her mother can also partly account for her "bossy" behaviors on unit, which similarly produce some of her outbursts.

B's intense guilt is clearly expressed in her drawing of herself, arms hidden behind her back. B hides the face of her sizzling anger at the unfairness with which she has been treated with the passive acceptance of her mother and struggles, often successfully (e.g. nearly normal Rorschach protocol), to present a smooth, round and innocuous front. At the same time, this aspect probably also expresses B's terror at being hurt again if she dares to open her arms to someone.

B's guilt also probably accounts for the recent emergence of self-harming impulses. In that regard, it appears likely that B inflicts pain on herself as a way of triggering a reaction from others (e.g. unit staff), which she then uses as a justification to act out her anger. By diluting the responsibility of the outburst and by experiencing actual pain, B both projects part of the guilt she experiences and physically atones for the remainder.

It is thought that the above dynamics offer a logical organization of the data and can account for most of B's observed behaviors but it remains questionable whether the occasional extreme intensity of such behaviors is not also fueled by a source other than ambivalence towards her mother. In this regard, and although there was very little evidence to support explicitly such a hypothesis, it is thought that abuse, most probably physical but also possibly sexual of B would provide a logical explanation for such intensity and perhaps as well for the nagging intensity of her guilt.

Psychotherapy should aim at verbalizing B's complex attachment to her biological mother. This work is likely to be long and difficult due to the oral, pre-verbal point of fixation and to the probable fantasized nature of this attachment. Letting B elaborate in a non-verbal manner and allusive manner on her history with her mother (e.g. play, drawings) is helpful by allowing material to flow out but change can only be obtained if such material is verbalized in details. Such verbalization can be done by B herself or by her therapist for her with similar effect.

B's love and anger, or hate for her mother equally need processing and it is by repeatedly allowing such opposed feelings to be expressed and verbally organized that B's ambivalence will eventually become more tolerable and generate less tension and acting-out behaviors. It is very likely that B will project her ambivalence onto her therapist and interpretation of any such transference reaction will most probably be extremely effective.

Once B's ambivalence will have been minimally processed and neutralized, her intense feelings of guilt should become readily accessible to therapeutic work, signaling the termination phase of her treatment.

B's foster-mother must be aware of B's guilt-ridden and ambivalent attachment to her biological mother because B is likely to react in an impulsive and probably very defensive and/or aggressive manner to any attempt at replacing her at this time. The fact that B's mother's parental rights have been terminated and that such termination was in part publicly endorsed by the mother is not relevant because B's attachment to her is rooted in her history and in her unconscious fantasies and therefore inaccessible to mere logic. Mothering B while she comes to term with her ambivalence and guilt is likely to be a long, frustrating and unrewarding way until B is ready to "open her arms" again. Temporary setbacks are also to be expected as B grows up and goes through adolescence.

On unit, it could be useful that both consequences and rewards be administered by a few (i.e. ideally one, realistically two or three) female staff and that each intervention be processed by presenting both aspects to B. For example, if B obtains a reward, the female family-teacher would praise her and explain that she would have given her a consequence as well if B's behaviors had been negative (the other way around in the case of a consequence). This may sound somewhat painstaking and self-evident but it is thought to be helpful in that, through repetition, it contributes to validating, processing and neutralizing B's ambivalence.

It is recommended to avoid rewarding B with oral gratifications (e.g. extra snack.) Offering a reward in the passive-oral realm reinforces B's regression to that level when she should be helped up to more advanced modes of relating to the world. This could also be processed with her, for example by saying "You're not a baby anymore and since you did so good, how about... (e.g. the two of us do something fun together)?"

When B exhibits self-harming behaviors, it is recommended to interpret to her that she might be trying to use staff's intervention as a pretext to act-out her anger and that there are other ways, more efficient and more mature to express such emotion (e.g. dancing to music in room, drawing angry faces, journal entry, processing with staff or therapist). As much as possible, it is recommended to avoid entering a physical confrontation with B following such attempt at self-harm for example by using natural consequences (e.g. time spent to care for the wound will have to be taken out of activity time, finger food.)

The possibility of abuse, physical and/or sexual must be kept in mind and will probably be more easily accessed and evaluated as B's memory is stimulated by psychotherapeutic work on her ambivalence.

Comment

This was the first evaluation I carried out in the facility following the blueprint described in introduction. I was therefore acting under the general, assumed, principle, that psychology would take over the conceptualization of the case with all needed resources and autonomy.

As I had finished testing and a good rapport had been established, B started to ask questions about what I knew about her life, to which I answered that I or anyone else didn't know much, due to the fact that her family had moved a lot and had not been very accessible or cooperative either. All I knew was in her social history. She nodded and asked if she could read this document.

At that point, I had a rough idea of what B's problems were and I knew that the disconnection between the first years of her life and her current placement, on her way to adoption contained very painful elements. Reading with me this short document was a way of providing her with a continuity and a relative objective truth that she had been denied. The adults working on her case, including her foster parents, treated her like a ten year old, which she was covertly angry about because it denied her history and her identity as mother-image that had provided her with the strength and courage to tolerate her predicament. A child she was indeed, and treating a child like one is a good thing, except that in B's case it also amounted to ignoring or denying her reality.

So I reviewed with B the social history section of her file. She was engrossed in the reading but was able to react in a very appropriate manner, occasionally very emotional. She was able to acknowledge several of her reported negative behaviors, while denying others. She was also able to acknowledge remembering parts of her erratic life but denied remembering others, particularly when abuse was involved, stating that she had a "memory problem".

Several issues triggered an outpour of sadness such as remembering her mother stating in the Court room that given the choice she would keep her oldest son against her and her younger brother, her father's lack of response to Human Services' request for a home-study and her "dumpster dives".

She later disclosed some of this information to her younger brother, which triggered a slew of indignation from the foster-parents and the Human Services worker. They would have preferred white lies and their anger was motivated by their unconscious fantasy of rescuing the little one, who was responding so well, against his mother's persona, nine year old B.

On the other hand, access to a truth was placing B in front of her hard reality, the first step towards accepting it. In last analysis, denying the truth to B was what directly triggered her explosion "out of nowhere".

Generally, the level of awareness of foster- or adoptive parents of their fantasy about fostering and adoption is dismal and other factors, most of them purely socio-cultural, often plainly discriminatory, dominate.

In many ways, the fostering of children resembles a self-proclaimed benevolent colonial power imposing its will, values, ways and version of history on a dominated people, allegedly for heir own good. The consequences are very often similar as well and can take the form of extreme rebellion.

B was eventually adopted by another family.

Survivor's Guilt

Seventeen, almost eighteen-year old boy. T and his twin brother were born to a single mother suffering from a serious psychiatric condition and were removed from her care when they were about three years of age, probably due to ongoing neglect. As a result of this original situation, nothing is known about pregnancy, birth, infancy or early childhood.

T's mother younger brother and his wife stepped up and fostered the boys until adoption was completed when they were about five years old.

T's parents' relationship, although stable appeared increasingly strained, possibly due to T's father having alcoholic tendencies and the couple eventually decided to attempt a fresh start in another State when the boys were about twelve. However, three years later, T's parents divorced and the boys followed their adoptive father back to their original State.

A few months later, without any clear reason or warning, T's twin brother killed himself with his rifle. T and his brother were home alone when this happened and T, upon hearing the gunshot discovered the body of his dead brother.

Reports converged to suggest that T's general attitude and behaviors significantly changed after this event and included frequent nightmares, self-abusive behaviors, suicidal statements, drug and alcohol use and outbursts of anger.

A return to his mother did not seem to alter his course and T's grades continued to plummet and his behaviors to degrade, with increased legal problems, which led to T's admission.

Primarily traumatic etiology, rooted in T's twin's suicide and the circumstances that accompanied his death. This event also probably had a stronger impact on T due to the loss of an entire pole of his existence (i.e. role distribution between twins.) It is likely that such twin-dynamic was also created and built around the brothers' early childhood with a disturbed and reputedly manic-depressive mother in an attempt at building and preserving an equilibrium in their lives.

It is therefore also safe to assume that a depressive streak might be present in T, as it was in his brother, although perhaps at a milder level, since his brother seemed to have endorsed the role of the protective and stabilizing element, thus denying expression to his own depressive state while allowing his brother to develop in a more worry-free manner.

The guilt perceived in T today, and a likely source to his own suicidal ideation, probably refers to his semi-conscious awareness of his brother's role in protecting him since early childhood and of his being oblivious to the cost. Incurred.

T's tense and compliant denial of any negative thoughts or feelings, as clearly illustrated in his results on the MACI, is seen more as an attempt at warding off potentially overwhelming emotions, perhaps in the fear that this would result in suicidality as well, rather than as a conscious attempt at deception, as seen in conduct disorders.

Now that his brother is not there to protect him, "who is going to?" is seen as the central question, going deep into his history and unconscious, to be addressed by T as he approaches adulthood and as the underlying meaning of his behavioral acting out since his brother's death. Such behaviors can be seen as a regressed, unconscious attempt at bringing his brother back, as T's behavioral escalation as his mother went to Las Vegas to get married can be seen as an unconscious attempt at bringing "Mommy" back as well.

Comment

As T's psychotherapist, I followed the lines of my own conceptualization. A few sessions were enough to bring up the twin dynamic and to discuss T's survivor's guilt, a concept he had not heard about. I had scenes of the movie "Ordinary People" running through my head.

I learned a lot about twins dynamic by questioning and listening to T about his relationship and history with his brother, which also helped to flesh out the missing boy and briefly and very minimally broach a few aspects of the traumatic situation of finding his dead body.

The repetition of negative behaviors as symbolic, magical, attempts at bringing him back was also laid out simply and straightforwardly.

T was discharged about six months after his admission. He obtained a degree in engineering a few years later.

Afterthought

Collating these vignettes, I realized that a large majority of them fell within the depressive spectrum and that nearly all presented a depressive aspect or layer. Most of these children had incurred a loss, not always real but always symbolic and acted out following different lines, depending on their specific histories and dynamics.

Nearly all of them as well began to exhibit symptoms or behaviors requiring close attention when they reached puberty or soon after, about thirteen years old for the girls and fourteen for the boys. This is most obviously due to the increased irritation put forth by hormonal changes and to the pressure to develop an identity on a sexual, relational and intellectual level.

The truth is that everybody hates to leave childhood behind at least until the advantages and rewards of autonomy begin to be realized, if they ever are. And even then.

The loss of childhood must be mourned at adolescence and for those who already have accumulated unprocessed losses this necessity quickly becomes overwhelming. Regression or denial springs up.

The most severe cases have never even reached the level where a loss can be grieved, however late, painfully, chronically or imperfectly.